INTRODUCTION

WHY CLEANSE?

The body is made up of approximately 150 trillion cells. Individual cells operate as miniature factories producing energy and raw materials to drive and build your body. Your body is under constant reconstruction. Every hour your body replaces 1 billion cells. Every seven years you have a brand new body. The burning of food to generate energy and raw materials for running and building the body generates metabolic waste that the body must dispose of through the elimination system.

Our bodies are designed to metabolize, cleanse, heal and repair on a daily basis. This will occur as long as we eat a diet high in fresh organic fruits, vegetables and seeds, as they are the natural detoxifiers for our body. It is equally as important to avoid unhealthy foods that deplete nutrient reserves required for health and generate toxic waste. Fresh fruits, vegetables and seeds provide us with high levels of vitamins, minerals, trace elements, enzymes, essential fatty acids and antioxidants required to bolster our cleansing and digestive systems.

INTRODUCTION

Most people do not eat enough of the right kinds of foods to facilitate a clean, well functioning body. Often times foods are consumed that create more toxic waste than the body can handle, resulting in toxic buildup. Symptoms which may indicate a long overdue and much needed cleanse include: a build up of fat located anywhere in the body (such as a liver roll around the upper abdomen or pot belly), cellulite, indigestion, reflux, gallstones, unstable blood sugar; cravings for sugar, alcohol, fatty fried or heavily salted food; depression, loss of energy and use of stimulants, parasites, headaches, reduced immune function, allergies, hormonal imbalances, constipation, diarrhea, hemorrhoids, cysts and other abnormal metabolism of fats including cholesterol and triglyceride issues.

The liver is the main fat burning organ in the body. It is like a built in dishwasher for detoxification purposes. The liver is also responsible for the regulation of fat metabolism as it can flush fat via the gallbladder into the small intestine. If the gallbladder is clear and there is adequate fiber available from the diet, excess fat is eliminated through the bowels. Very often the liver is congested and the gallbladder is blocked. Sugar and processed foods are the main culprits for degenerating organs and jamming functioning systems. Gallstones are formed from mucus (sugar), surrounded by hardened layers of cholesterol, unabsorbed and misplaced minerals and salts. Gallstones are geometric in shape, which easily fit together and pack tightly into the gallbladder. Stones or gravel develop and accumulate over time, blocking the essential flow of bile, resulting in toxic build up and a reduction in quality of health.

After World War II the "Chemical Revolution" began. Since that time we have been introduced and exposed to over 2 million new toxic synthetic substances also known as zenobiotics. Multiple daily exposures of zenobiotics come from myriad of sources and are known carcinogens. They are also responsible for many auto-immune diseases, allergies of all kinds

INTRODUCTION

including environmental sensitivities and increase the aging process. Here are a few examples of zenobiotics: Chemically produced conventional food, processed foods of every kind, air and water pollution, chemical cleaning products, office supplies, synthetic personal care products, out-gassing from carpets, paints and fabrics on furniture and lawn care products such as fertilizers and weed killers just to mention a few. There are two ways you can address zenobiotics. One of the best solutions is to minimize exposure to toxic substances by avoiding them as much as possible. The other way is to eat organic nutrient-rich food that supplies your liver with specific and adequate nutrients to support the detoxification process known as Phase One and Phase Two Biotransformation. Harmful fat-soluble zenobiotic substances can be broken down and eliminated from the body, if there is an abundance of available nutrients and the detoxification pathways are balanced. If there are not enough nutrients to support the liver's detoxification process then these harmful external toxic substances are stored in fat tissues and become internal toxic substances that continually poison the body and generate disease. The body is smart and as a defense mechanism it makes fat cells to store zenobiotics away from vital organs, such as the brain, heart, lungs and liver. If toxins can not be eliminated via the liver's detoxification pathways more fat cells are generated and more zenobiotics are placed in storage. The Power of Chow 14-Day Gourmet Cleanse & Rejuvenation Program provides the body with a surplus of specific and adequate nutrients to support the cleansing process.

Most people want to detoxify and cleanse their body, however many methods require fasting which often depletes energy levels and may cause undesirable side effects. Using gourmet organic fresh foods for a two-week period will support and improve liver health and function. The liver is responsible for over 150 physiological processes that are directly connected to our overall health. Most of the recipes are quick, easy to prepare and can be used as grab and go

INTRODUCTION

food, to accommodate a busy lifestyle. This dietary cleansing program is designed for a two-week period. Unlike most cleansing programs which promote fasting on water, juices or other drinks, this cleanse utilizes whole organic fresh foods prepared in gourmet style to provide the body with high quality, live nutrients that simultaneously detoxify, balance and heal. It is very beneficial for people who want to maintain their energy level and their busy lifestyle while cleansing their body. Every recipe will help strengthen your digestive system. Many people show a reduction in weight because nutrient levels are high enough to shut off the hunger mechanism. When addictive foods are avoided and nutrient requirements are met, the normal response is to stop eating.

During The Power Of Chow, 14-day Gourmet Cleanse & Rejuvenation Program you will avoid eating the following: Over cooked foods, meat, fish, fowl, grains and all grain products, soy and all soy products (except miso and nama shoyu soy sauce), legumes, all processed and packaged foods, pasteurized dairy products (including cheese, milk, eggs, yogurt) and conventional produce. Many foods listed above are healthy options (everything that is not processed or pasteurized); however for our cleansing purposes they are inappropriate. The goal is to get more alkaline foods and minerals into your body to neutralize metabolic acid waste. In addition The Power of Chow 14-Day Gourmet Cleanse & Rejuvenation Program supplies specific nutrients which reduce fat soluble chemical toxins, stored in fat tissues, into less harmful substances that can be eliminated from the body.

TABLE OF CONTENTS

INTRODUCTION
- Why Cleanse? 2
- Table of Contents 6

CHAPTER ONE
Things to Know Ahead Of Time:
- *Organic vs. Non-Organic Produce* 12
- *Fruit & Vegetable Cleaning* 12
- *Before Handling Food* 14
- *Purified Water* 14

CHAPTER TWO
- Gourmet Cleanse Tips 16

CHAPTER THREE
- Most Often Asked Questions 20

CHAPTER FOUR
- Getting Started 26
  - *Snacks* 26
  - *Digestion Notes* 29
  - *Recipe Notes* 29
  - *Food For Thought* 29
  - *Base Shopping List* 30
  - *Detox Smoothie Shopping List* 31
  - *Day 1 Lunch Shopping List* 32
  - *Day 1 Dinner Shopping List* 32
  - *Things To Do Daily* 33
  - *Pre-Breakfast, Days 1-14* 33

TABLE OF CONTENTS

CHAPTER FIVE

Day 1-14 Gourmet Cleanse Recipes 34
    Green Detox Smoothie, Breakfast, Days 1-14 35
        Day 1 Lunch 36
            Cream of Asparagus Soup 36
            Avocado Kale Salad 37
Food Preparation Note:
    Day 1 Dinner
        Day 2 Shopping List 38

Day 1 Dinner/Day 2 Lunch 39
    Salad Extraordinaire with Miso Salad Dressing
        Salad Extraordinaire 40
        Sesame Miso Salad Dressing 41
Food Preparation Note:
    Day 2 Dinner/Day 3 Lunch
        No Shopping Today 42

Day 2 Dinner/Day 3 Lunch 43
    Italian Wild Rice & Marinated Collard Greens
        Italian Wild Rice 44
        Marinated Collard Greens (see food preparation note on page 42)
Food Preparation Note:
    Day 3 Dinner/4 Lunch
        Shopping List Day 3 46

Day 3 Dinner/Day 4 Lunch 47
    Miso Vegetable Soup & Quick Onion Crackers
        Miso Vegetable Soup 48
Food Preparation Note:
    Day 4 Dinner/Day 5 Lunch

TABLE OF CONTENTS

Shopping List Day 4 50
Day 4 Dinner/Day 5 Lunch 51
    Quinoa Tabouli & Romaine Lettuce
    Quinoa Tabouli 52
Food Preparation Note:
    No Food Preparation Today
    Shopping List, Day 5 54

Day 5 Dinner/Day 6 Lunch 55
    Arame Salad, Ginger Tahini Miso Dressing with Mixed Green Salad & Avocado
    Arame Salad 56
    Ginger Tahini Miso Dressing 57
Food Preparation Note:
    Day 6 Dinner/Day 7 Lunch
    Shopping List, Day 6 58

Day 6 Dinner/Day 7 Lunch 59
    Teriyaki Pate Nori Rolls, Ginger Tahini Miso Dipping Sauce
    Teriyaki Pate 60
    Teriyaki Pate & Nori Rolls 61
Food Preparation Note:
    No Food Preparation Today
    Shopping List Day 7 62

Day 7 Dinner/Day 8 Lunch 63
    Red Pepper Cilantro Soup with Bib Lettuce Rolls/Feta Cheese
    Red Pepper Cilantro Soup 64
    Bib Lettuce Rolls/Feta Cheese 65

TABLE OF CONTENTS

Food Preparation Note:
    Day 8 Dinner/Day 9 Lunch
        Shopping List Day 8 66

Day 8 Dinner/ Day 9 Lunch 67
    Jalapeño Pumpkin Beet Green Enchiladas
        Jalapeño Pumpkin Pate Recipe 68
        Fresh Salsa 69
        Guacamole 70

Food Preparation Note:
    Day 9 Dinner/Day 10 Lunch
        Shopping list Day 9 72

Day 9 Dinner/Day 10 Lunch 73
    Stuffed Grape Leaves, Greek Salad with Fresh Dill Dijon
        Stuffed Grape Leaves 74
        Greek Salad 75
        Fresh Dill Dijon 76

Food Preparation Note:
    No Food Preparation Today
        Shopping List Day 10 78

Day 10 Dinner/Day 11 Lunch 79
    Zucchini Noodles with Pesto Sauce & Caesar Salad
        Zucchini Noodles with Pesto Sauce 80
        Caesar Salad 81

Food Preparation Note:
    Day 11 Dinner/Day 12 Lunch
        Shopping List, Day 11 82

TABLE OF CONTENTS

Day 11 Dinner/Day 12 Lunch 83
    Thai Stir Fry over Wild Rice
        Thai Stir Fry 84
        Thai Stir Fry Sauce 85
Food Preparation Note:
    Day 12 Dinner/Day 13 Lunch
        Shopping List Day 12 86

Day 12 Dinner/Day 13 Lunch 87
    Mexican-Hummus, Fresh Salsa & Guacamole
        Mexican-Hummus 88
Food Preparation Note:
    Day 13 Dinner/Day 14 Lunch
        Shopping List Day 13 90

Day 13 Dinner/Day 14 Lunch 91
    Marinara Sauce with Wild Rice & Wilted Spinach Salad
        Marinara Sauce 92
        Wilted Spinach Salad 93
Food Preparation Note:
    Day 14 Dinner
        Shopping List Day 14 94

Day 14 Dinner 95
    Savory Herbed Wild Rice, Whipped Cauliflower with Mushroom Gravy Extraordinaire
        Savory Herb Wild Rice 96
        Whipped Cauliflower 97
        Mushroom Gravy 98

Congratulations! 99

TABLE OF CONTENTS

CHAPTER SIX
More Recipes

Cracker Recipes 101
    Quick Onion Crackers 102
    Herbal Flax Crackers 103

Fermented Drinks 105
    Sprouting Process 106
    Rejuvelac 107
    Lemon Fruit Rejuvenade 108
    Frozen Lime Mint Rejuvenade 109

Desserts 111
    Berry pie 112
    Fudgy Carob or Chocolate Fondue 113
    Almond Balls 114
    Mango Pudding 115

Glossary 117

CHAPTER ONE

THINGS TO KNOW AHEAD OF TIME

Organic vs. Non-Organic Produce

Buy organic produce and products as often as possible for all of the recipes. Studies show that nutrient levels are higher and you are not exposing yourself, your family or the Earth to dangerous toxic chemicals. If you live in an area that does not supply organic produce or you have limited funds, do the best you can. Wash produce before using not before storing to decrease spoilage time. Here is a recipe for making your own vegetable wash at home:

Fruit & Vegetable Cleaning

Fruit and vegetable wash recipe for soaking: This recipe is for lettuce, spinach and other leafy greens. Remove and discard outer leaves of leafy greens, including cabbage before using. Don't over soak. Three minutes is a good amount of time for all leafy greens. This recipe works well for grapes, broccoli, cauliflower and other hard to wash items. Fill a small plastic tub half full of cold water. Add ¼ cup white vinegar, 2 T. salt, 1 T. baking soda to the tub. Soak your fruits or vegetables, non-leafy greens for three to five minutes and then rinse well (approximately one minute) under cold water. Fruit and vegetable wash recipe for spray bottles: This recipe works for vegetables and fruits that you are washing one at a time, such as cucumbers or zucchini. Gently mix together one cup of water, two tablespoons of baking soda, 1 T. lemon juice and 20 drops of grapefruit seed extract (can be purchased at the health food store or ordered on line). Pour into spray bottle. After spraying your fruits or vegetables, rub the solution gently around the surface and then let them sit for approximately two minutes. Rinse well (approximately one minute) with cold water. Carrots, beets, celery, squash and other produce can be scrubbed with a vegetable brush, after spraying and while rinsing with cold water. This applies to melons and squash to prevent bacteria from entering the fruit, when it is cut. Mushrooms should not be soaked, as they absorb water. Dampen a paper towel with cold water and wipe them clean.

Foods with the highest levels of pesticides:

Fruits
- Peaches
- Apples
- Strawberries
- Nectarines
- Pears
- Cherries
- Red Raspberries
- Grapes

Vegetables
- Spinach
- Bell Peppers
- Hot Peppers
- Celery
- Potatoes

THINGS TO KNOW AHEAD OF TIME

Before handling Food:
Make sure to wash your hands with non-toxic, not anti-microbial soap. Dr. Bronner's Natural soap is one I like and recommend to my clients. Clean counter tops ahead of time. You may use equal amounts of white vinegar and water in a spray bottle or purchase a natural cleaning product such as Meyers. DO NOT wash produce with detergent or bleach solutions. Fruits and vegetables are porous and can absorb the detergent or bleach, which is not intended for use on foods. Consuming them on fruits and vegetables have the potential to make you sick.

Purified Water
It is important to drink spring water or purified water when ever possible. Tap water has been treated with toxic substances. Avoid buying water in plastic bottles as they contain toxic substances that leach into the water. The plastic bottles are polluting the Earth including our land fills and the oceans. You may need to purchase reusable non-polycarbonate bottles and get them filled at your local health food store. Another option is to have water delivered to you, unless you have a good filtering system on your faucet. I encourage you to use non-contaminated water whenever preparing your food as well. This would include soaking and rinsing nuts and seeds. If you do not have a filter on your sink, then I suggest you soak your nuts and seeds in purified water and then use your tap water for rinsing, to keep the cost down. In the long run, it may save you time and money to purchase a good filtration system. I always recommend doing the best you can in any situation and if a Brita pitcher is what you can afford then purchase it.

NOTES

CHAPTER TWO

GOURMET CLEANSE TIPS

1. Eat only when you are hungry. Look and smell the food before you eat. This turns on digestive juices which activates digestion and increases assimilation of nutrients. Close your eyes, take a few deep breaths, give your abdominal area a few gentle rubs and smile internally. Send good feelings and thoughts to your belly and think about how important it is to nourish yourself. A happy belly increases digestive power and the bio-availability of nutrients. This means you'll eat less and receive more!

2. Bless your food and feel gratitude for the beautiful meal or snack you are about to ingest. Above all take time to enjoy your food and nourish yourself.

3. Eat slowly, chew your food well and mix the saliva into the food or drink you are eating. Pay attention to how delicious and energizing the food is. Relaxing while eating and chewing food completely is the number 1 rule for building the digestive system. Proper chewing breaks the food down into smaller particles releasing and activating food enzymes found in live food. Digestive enzymes found in saliva aid in pre-digestion, so it is easier on the system to get the nutrition from what you're eating. Every cell, tissue and system in your body is dependent on the digestive system for sustenance and vitality. This process is powerful and so simple that we often overlook it.

4. Always eat when you are relaxed so your body can focus on digestion. When you are experiencing stress your body can not make HCL or digestive enzymes which digest your food. Most people spend over 80% of their body's energy digesting overly-cooked and processed food. This leaves only 20% remaining energy for rejuvenating the body and day to day living. When you eat enzyme nutrient-rich live food these numbers invert and your body has 80% of its energy delegated to rejuvenation and leading a healthy active life.

5. If you are feeling stressed and you need to nourish yourself with food, Try This: Close your eyes, place your hands and your attention on your stomach. Take 10 slow, deep belly breaths. Eat slowly and continue to breathe and relax.

6. Be prepared ahead of time with your food plan and your shopping list. You know you will be hungry every day and that you will need to eat. This is not a surprise and happens many times per day. One scenario is to wait until hunger arrives, blood sugar levels drop and foggy thinking sets in. This leads to unconscious eating of what ever is available. The other option, which is always the best, is to be prepared, with snacks, meal planning and shopping.

7. Keep an on going shopping list and make a note when you are low or have run out of staples in your kitchen.

GOURMET CLEANSE TIPS

8. Add items to your grocery list if you want to make a new recipe. Shopping lists save you time and money at the store. If you always have one going, you'll get used to taking ingredient inventory which will aid in menu planning and shopping.

9. Before going to bed at night, read over your menu plan for the next day. It only takes a couple of minutes to soak and rinse seeds, nuts or sprouts.

10. Keep things simple if you need to. Tailor your diet/menu plan so that you are not overwhelmed. This is essential in the beginning. Do what you can as you go along. If you are following The Power Of Chow 14-Day Gourmet Cleanse & Rejuvenation Program and you don't have time to make what is on the menu, feel free to make a salad, add some avocado and sprinkle in some wild rice. Keep it simple when you need to. Double recipes so you have leftovers for additional meals. It's fun to make food with friends or setup a food exchange so you get a variety. This can also save you and your friends food preparation time.

11. Take time on a day off to prepare things that will last for a longer period of time. Examples: Crackers, soaked/dried seeds and nuts, wild rice, quinoa, marinated vegetables.

12. Allow 3-4 hours between eating and bedtime. Some people have very high metabolisms and may need something to eat to help them rest. If you are one of these people, allow 1-2 hours between eating and bedtime. Avoid eating or drinking sweets (desserts) at bedtime to keep blood sugar levels stable. A shredded apple with cinnamon and 2 T. of plain yogurt is a good idea if eating before bed. Grapefruit with romaine lettuce is another good snack between the last meal and bedtime because romaine lettuce provides chromium which stabilizes blood sugar. Keep in mind that human growth hormone (HGH) is secreted while we sleep. These hormones support youth and vitality. Deep physiological processes that cleanse and restore are simultaneously happening while sleeping. If your body is busy digesting food the rejuvenation process during deep sleep is diminished.

13. Make sure to get adequate sleep. Go to bed at the same time every night, if possible, and get up at the same time everyday. Set daily lifestyle practices. Sleep and eat at the same time everyday. This practice will help to stabilize the endocrine and elimination systems. I recommend going to bed as early as 9:00 PM and before 11 PM. The liver begins cleaning the blood at 11 PM. That's a big job that needs to happen while sleeping. Every hour you sleep before midnight is equal to getting 2 hours of sleep.

14. When you wake up in the morning. Take several deeps breathes and stretch before getting out of bed. Look for beauty in the room around you. Feel your body, smile at your self, internally, and then smile at the world around you. Be grateful for the day ahead. Set your intention for peaceful thoughts and positive communication with others avoiding unnecessary stress. Stay connected to yourself and committed to your healthy lifestyle practice. Teach yourself to be solution oriented. Breathe deeply through any stressful situations, encounters or challenges.

15. Nourishment comes in many forms. Oxygen is the 1 source of sustenance. Without air we die in 3 minutes. Without water we die in 3 days and in 3 weeks without food. Breathe deeply, through out the day. Breathing is free and full of life giving energy. Breathing supports peaceful thoughts, clear thinking and a deeper connection to ourselves and the world around us.

CHAPTER THREE

MOST OFTEN ASKED QUESTIONS

Question: *What are enzyme inhibitors?*
Answer: Enzyme Inhibitors are toxic substances found in grains, seeds, nuts and legumes which suppress digestion. Enzyme inhibitors prevent these foods from sprouting in the Fall season, when they are on the ground. Enzyme inhibitors allow seeds to lay dormant during the Winter season, protecting them from freezing temperatures. In the Spring time the rain dissolves the enzyme inhibitors allowing the seed to sprout. When seeds are sprouted the enzyme potential is increased and proteins are converted into amino acids, carbohydrates are converted into simple starches/sugars and fats are converted into essential fatty acids. This maximizes digestion as the food is in predigested form. Enzyme inhibitors protect the species from being overly consumed by animals in the wild, because they are toxic and difficult to digest. Animals intuitively know this when they eat them. Many enzyme inhibitors found in beans and grains are very toxic and can cause illness. Soaking, sprouting and cooking

inactivate enzyme inhibitors and increases their nutrient bio-availability. Heat over 120 degrees destroys enzyme inhibitors as well as enzymes.

• • • • • • • • • • • • •

Question: *Why are Enzymes important?*
Answer: There are 3 different types of enzymes. Enzymes that come in live or raw food, digestive enzymes predominantly made in the pancreas and metabolic enzymes that act as catalysts which are used in every function of the body, including all healing and repairing. You could not blink your eye without a metabolic enzyme. When we eat enzyme rich foods digestion is enhanced and the body is not required to make digestive enzymes. The body can focus energy on the production of metabolic enzymes which sustain health, vitality and proper physiological function. This is where you gain the 80% energy increase from eating live raw food.

• • • • • • • • • • • • •

Question: *How long do I soak nuts and seeds?*
Answer: Sesame seeds that have the hull removed do not need to be soaked. Pine nuts do not have many enzyme inhibitors so they do not need to be soaked, unless you want to remove some of the oil. Cashews are not truly raw because they are found on the inside of a toxic fruit and heat has been used to remove them. Buckwheat only needs 4 hours of soaking time, however it's ok if you soak it for 6 hours. Quinoa, amaranth and wild rice need 8 hours of soak time. Flax seeds do not need to be soaked unless you are making crackers and you want them to provide the gelatinous substance for binding purposes. You can soak flax seeds for 30 minutes to 8 hours depending on the recipe. Hemp seeds and chia seeds do not need soaking. Chia seeds contain a gel like substance called hylauronic acid that holds 9 times the

amount of liquid. This gel is very healing to the entire GI tract. Soak pumpkin and sunflower seeds, almonds, Brazil nuts and macadamia nuts for 8 hours. Soak walnuts and pecans for 4-6 hours as they are softer and do not require the full 8 hours to remove the enzyme inhibitors. Soak seeds and nuts individually in uncovered jars.

• • • • • • • • • • • • •

Question: *Should I use bottled water to soak seeds and nuts?*
Answer: If you have filtered water I suggest you use it for the soaking and rinsing process. If you only have bottled water I recommend you soak them in the bottled water and do your rinsing from regular water as it could get very expensive to use it for both processes. Always do the best you can when it comes to using purified water. Avoid purchasing plastic water bottles as our oceans and landfills are overflowing with plastic.

• • • • • • • • • • • • •

Question: *After I have soaked the seeds/nuts what's next?*
Answer: The soak water will be cloudy from the enzyme inhibitors. Drain off the soaking water either by using a colander, a strainer or cheese cloth. Make sure you rinse the seeds/nuts very well and then use them for your recipe or store them covered in the refrigerator until you are ready to use them.

• • • • • • • • • • • • •

Question: *How long will they last in the refrigerator?*
Answer: Most nuts and seeds last in the refrigerator for four to five days, if sealed properly. Before using, always check to make sure they are consumable. You don't want any mold or fungus growing on them. Wild rice will last in the refrigerator for approximately ten days, however you must make sure

to look at it after a week. There should be no fuzz growing on the outside and it should not smell sour.

• • • • • • • • • • • • •

Question: *How long do the smoothies last if they are refrigerated?*
Answer: I recommend you make fresh smoothies every day as the nutrients start to oxidize. If you have a smoothie left over you may store it overnight in a covered container and consume it the next day, however fresh is always better. If you don't have time to prepare your smoothie in the morning it's better to make it at night and store it in the refrigerator, than to not have it at all.

• • • • • • • • • • • • •

Question: *How long do the prepared recipes last as leftovers?*
Answer: The recipes I have chosen do well in the refrigerator overnight, unless I indicate otherwise, such as salads with dressing, cut tomatoes or guacamole. Most pates, wild rice dishes, desserts and soups will last 2-3 days. Salad dressings will last approximately 7 days. Crackers that have been dehydrated and are stored properly will last close to 6 months, if they are refrigerated. Energy balls that are refrigerated will last approximately 6 months.

• • • • • • • • • • • • •

Question: *Do I have to stick to the menu or if I get rushed can I just eat a salad or fresh fruit?*
Answer: You can always improvise when it's necessary. Stressing over meal preparation is not helpful when you are trying to cleanse your body as it creates more acid waste that must be removed by using alkaline minerals. I keep pre-soaked wild rice, avocados and plenty of raw vegetables and fruit on hand for quick easy snacks and meals. You can always make a delicious salad to replace any meal on the menu and your cleanse will not be interupted.

MOST OFTEN ASKED QUESTIONS

Question: *Can I mix the menu plan around to suit my schedule?*
Answer: Yes, you can. I recommend that you start every day with the fresh detox smoothie as this will jump start your day with nutrient-rich food that will support the cleansing process and give you plenty of energy to live your life.

• • • • • • • • • • • • •

Question: *Can I skip meals and snacks if I'm not hungry?*
Answer: You should always listen to your body and not eat unless you are hungry. Some people are not hungry first thing in the morning and need to exercise prior to eating. This is OK. Listen to your body. I recommend you prepare and drink the detox smoothie everyday, as it supplies your body with essential nutritional requirements for cleansing. Skip snacks if you are not hungry. If you want to make a smoothie for dinner instead of making a meal, that is OK too, just make sure you include an abundance of fresh greens for cleansing. If you are going to skip a meal, skip dinner and then make your smoothie for breakfast. It's always better to consume your food earlier in the day than later, when digestion is strong.

• • • • • • • • • • • • •

Question: *What kind of a blender do I need?*
Answer: I recommend the Vita-Mix 5200 which is a high performance multi-purpose blender. It has the power to quickly breakdown leafy greens such as kale and spinach so you get a creamy smooth texture for your smoothies, soups and sauces. It also has a variable speed control that easily chops vegetables and fruits into small pieces that create varying textures. The container is BPA toxin-free with a soft-grip handle and a tight fitting lid that is easy to remove. It comes with a 7-year warranty. To learn more go to www.thepowerofchow.com

MOST OFTEN ASKED QUESTIONS

Question: *Do I need a dehydrator and if so which one do you recommend?*
Answer: Most of the recipes do not require a dehydrator. There are cracker recipes that can be low-temperature baked if your oven setting allows you to adjust it to 120 degrees or lower. Some ovens will not adjust below 170 degrees. If you have one of these ovens you can still use it to make crackers however you will need to get a thermometer and regulate the temperature by setting the oven on it's lowest setting and leaving the oven door open. The dehydrator I recommend is the Excalibur brand. These dehydrators come in various sizes and are easy to use as they have front loading trays. If you are not ready to purchase a dehydrator use your oven. If you are interested in purchasing an excalibur dehydrator you can contact us at www.thepowerofchow.com and we can assist you with placing your order.

• • • • • • • • • • • • • •

Question: *I notice the term pulse-chop used in many of the recipes, what does that term mean?*
Answer: Pulse-Chop is used to reference a preparation method using the Cuisinart Food Processor with the S-blade. This method is achieved by rapidly pressing the pulse-button control several times until you reach the desired texture. This reduces the amount of time you spend in the kitchen as you can chop many vegetables, fruits, and herbs very quickly.

• • • • • • • • • • • • • •

Question: *Will I experience adverse side effects while detoxing?*
Answer: Experience is individual, depending on their health, body type and previous dietary habits. For example someone who drinks coffee daily may experience headaches when they stop. Typically the headaches subside after 3 days on this cleanse. If your previous diet was high in processed foods you may want to approach this dietary cleanse at a slower rate, which gives your body time to adapt. Begin with the Green Detox smoothie daily, eliminate processed foods and slowly introduce some of the recipes in this book. For more questions and answers visit our website at www.thepowerofchow.com

CHAPTER FOUR

GETTING STARTED

Snacks

You may choose to eat a mid-morning and/or mid-afternoon snack. Only eat if you are hungry and stop eating at the first signal of feeling full. Keep in mind it's good to eat protein, fat and carbohydrates every time you eat so your body feels balanced. When you eat balanced meals and snacks your body will feel satiated, eliminating undesirable food cravings.

Here are some ideas: Raw fruit such as apples, oranges, grapefruit, berries (of any variety), kiwi, pears, bananas, avocado, papaya, mango, apricots, plums and grapes call all be eaten with hempnut seeds, raw spinach or romaine lettuce. Melons can be used as a snack option, however they are the exception to the rule. Consume melon alone as it does not digest well with most other foods. Goat yogurt with fruit and a few sprinkles of seeds or almonds, raisins or goji berries makes a satisfying snack. Eating celery or romaine lettuce with fruit aids in

GETTING STARTED - SNACKS

digestion and balances blood sugar levels so you have longer sustained energy through out the day without feeling tired. Hemp nut seeds provide 11 grams of protein in a ¼ cup, plus EFA's and are easy to travel with. They are satisfying and can be eaten with a piece of fruit or sprinkled into yogurt. Chia seeds can be stirred into yogurt with fruit for a balanced snack.

Raw veggies such as carrots, celery, cucumber, romaine lettuce, cherry tomatoes, sugar snap peas or shelled peas, raw baby peppers of various colors or red, green or yellow peppers (sliced) are all delicious snacks. Seed and nut pates found on page 60 and 68 can be prepared and used as snack options with vegetables. A slice of raw cheese or a teaspoon of raw nut butter is a good snack to combine with fruits or vegetables.

Another snack you can easily make is the Miso Soup Broth recipe on page 49. Keep it simple and pulse-chop some scallions, parsley or cilantro and/or garlic into it after you have the base blended. Miso broth provides a source of B vitamins. Miso is a fermented soy bean paste which supports friendly bacteria in your colon. The almond butter supplies protein and fat. Garlic, onions, parsley and cilantro add extra nutrients that support nourishment and cleansing.

Dried fruit is a good dessert option, however it is more concentrated in sugar, so avoid it if you have Candida, blood sugar imbalances, weight loss or weight maintenance concerns. You can combine it with seed or nut butters to add the protien and fat for a balanced snack. You may eat raw energy balls as a dessert or snack option too. Make sure you don't over eat them as they are very rich in carbohydrates. If you don't burn the energy it gets stored as fat. The recipe is located in the last section listed under Desserts. Dried fruit and other varieties of sweet fruit, eaten too close to bedtime will supply high carbohydrate energy and may create

GETTING STARTED

sleep disturbances. This is the best reason for consuming desserts and sweet snacks earlier in the day. Allow 3-4 hours in between eating and going to sleep. When you go to sleep on an empty stomach, it allows the internal body Ph to become alkaline, which is essential for cleaning, healing and repairing. If the body has to digest food when you are sleeping, sleep cycles are interrupted and rejuvenation work is reduced. Some people say they cannot sleep if their stomach is empty or that they get to hungry between their last meal of the day and bedtime. If this is an issue for you then I suggest you eat romaine lettuce with a grapefruit or an apple. Grapefruit is low in sugar, high in vitamin C and alkalizing. Romaine lettuce provides chromium for stabilizing your blood sugar levels. Nuts and seeds are a good snack choice as they contain protein, fat and carbohydrates, so you feel full and nourished after eating a small amount. Make sure they have been soaked in purified water to remove the toxic enzyme inhibitors, prior to eating. There is no need to soak hemp nut seeds. For more information please review the section on "Things To Know Ahead of Time", or "Most Often Asked Questions" located in the front of the book. Keep in mind that seeds are easier to digest than nuts so include more seeds in your diet than nuts. I would recommend consuming more hemp nuts, sesame seeds, pumpkin seeds, chia seeds as a first choice, followed by almonds. Walnuts, cashews, pine nuts, Brazil nuts and pecans should be eaten in smaller amounts, as eating too many nuts can be difficult for the liver/gallbladder to process.

A live cracker with cheese or low-temperature prepared granola with fruit provides a satisfying on the go snack. Raw energy bars, raw goat cheese, goat yogurt, or raw nut butters are available in most health food stores.

Digestion Notes

If your goal is to lose or maintain weight make sure you eat smaller amounts of cheese, nuts, crackers and dried fruit. Consume more fresh veggies and fruit, with hemp, chia, sunflower or pumpkin seeds. Digestion is stronger in the later morning, mid-day and early evening hours before 5pm. Eat more food earlier in the day and eat light at night. Chew more, enjoy more, nourish more, eat less, and live longer.

Recipe Notes

Amounts make approximately 4 servings. Each night, when you prepare your dinner, there should be enough left over for the next day's lunch. Please adjust the recipe to fit your dietary requirements. If you are preparing these recipes only for yourself, you'll want to decrease the amounts.

Food for Thought

You may already have many of the items on the shoping list, while others you may need to purchase. If you are unfamilar with an item on the list, most employees in the health food stores are knowledgeable and can assist you or visit our website. We are happy to answer your questions or you can email us at askeloise@thepowerofchow.com Please note that for your convenience daily shopping lists are provided. Spending money on high quality food to nourish yourself and your family is one of the golden keys to a long successful life. Investing in your health is the best investment you will ever make in your life.

GETTING STARTED - SHOPPING LIST

Base Shopping List

Commonly used items through out the Gourmet Cleanse
Coconut Oil (cold pressed, non-hydrogenated)
Olive Oil
Apple Cider Vinegar (unpasteurized and unfiltered is best)
Nama Shoyu (unpasteurized soy sauce)
Garlic, Fresh
Red Onions, 2
Lemons, 4
Limes, 2
Chia Seeds, 8-16 ounces
Wild Rice, organic, hand harvested, hard husk removed www.thepowerofchow.com
Agave or Raw Honey
Hemp Nut Seeds
Goji Berries
Sunflower Seeds, 3 cups
Pumpkin Seeds, 3 cups
Almond Butter, raw
Tahini, raw
Miso paste, light and dark red, unpasteurized
Quinoa
Sea Salt (Himalayan Salt or Celtic Sea Salt)
Herbamare Seasoning Salt
Cumin, dried
Cayenne Pepper
Ripe Avocados, 4-6

GETTING STARTED - SHOPPING LIST

Detox Smoothie Shopping List

1 bunch Bananas, 6-8

Apples, 4-6

Pears, 4-6

Strawberries, Blueberries, Raspberries (fresh or frozen is OK for smoothies)

Spinach, 1 head or package of pre-washed baby Spinach

Kale, Dinosaur (Lacinata)

Coconut Water, 4-6 containers or Rejuvelac

Hemp Protein Powder, organic

Cinnamon

Cardamom

GETTING STARTED - SHOPPING LIST

Day One Shopping List

Lunch: Cream of Asparagus Soup with Avocado Kale Salad
Asparagus or Spinach
Shallots or Avocado (you will need extra if you are making the spinach soup)
Dinosaur Kale, 1 bunch
Cherry Tomatoes, 1 basket or 2 cups
Avocados, 1 ripe

Dinner: Salad Extraordinaire & Sesame Miso Salad Dressing
Mixed Greens, 4 cups
Celery, 1 bunch
Fennel, 1 bulb
Burdock Root, 1, 3-inch stalk
Cilantro, 1 bunch
Spinach, 1 bunch (also on your smoothie list)
Arame Seaweed, 1 package
Walnuts, ½ cup soaked or 1/3 cup Hemp Nut Seeds, not soaked
Feta Cheese, optional, or some other raw cheese
Basil, one bunch fresh or 1 jar, dried
Oregano, one bunch fresh, or 1 jar, dried

Things To Do Daily

- Every morning you will be preparing a "Green Detox" smoothie for breakfast and for your mid-morning snack.

- Every day you will be preparing enough food at dinner time for the next day's lunch (to save you money, time and provide you with nutritious meals).

- Always check the Food Preparation note at the end of each dinner meal for instructions on what you need to prepare for the following night, although some nights there is no preparation required.

- Make sure to update your shopping list so you are prepared.

Pre-Breakfast Days 1-14

Each day, begin with eight ounces of room temperature purified water, adding ¼-½ lemon, hand-squeezed. Lemon provides vitamin C which boosts the immune system and assists the body with removing metabolic waste. Drink green tea or Yerba Mate. Green tea is energizing and loaded with nutrients that are alkalizing (cleansing) to the body. Yerba Mate provides a natural source of chromium, which stabilizes blood sugar. You may sweeten your tea with raw agave, honey or stevia.

CHAPTER FIVE

Day 1-14 Gourmet Cleanse Recipes

BREAKFAST
GREEN DETOX SMOOTHIE

Every time you eat, sit down, breathe, relax, take your time and enjoy! Drink liquids slowly, holding every mouthful for 30 seconds while you mix the saliva into the drink. Chew your liquids. Mixing saliva into each mouthful will aid in the digestive process and increase assimilation of nutrients. This technique is one of the essential tools you can use for building a powerful digestive system. You will get more nutrients from your food and you will support your elimination system. When you eat and drink slowly, you give your stomach time to signal or register fullness in the brain. This shuts off the appetite at the appropriate time so you stop eating when you are full. It is critical to listen to your body and to stop eating when you feel the first signal of fullness in your stomach. Overeating (even good healthy food) over-burdens the digestive system, slows down metabolism and eventually destroys the body's natural ability to digest food and assimilate nutrients.

BREAKFAST
Green Detox Smoothie

Green Detox Smoothie

1 Banana

1 Pear, any kind, however ripe Bosc pears are delicious

1 Apple

2 T. Hemp Protein Powder, rounded

2 T. Chia Seeds, rounded

2 T. Coconut Oil, rounded

2 cups Coconut Water and/or Purified Water

1 tightly packed cup of Spinach

2 large sprigs Dinosaur Kale

1 t. Cinnamon

1 t. Cardamom

> Coconut Water is nature's natural sports drink as it contains valuable sources of electrolytes that detox and hydrate the body. These include, calcium, magnesium, sodium and potassium.

Place: cut-up fruit into the blender. Cover with liquid and add the chia seeds. Blend until smooth. Allow mixture to sit for 1 or 2 minutes while the chia seeds gel and are absorbed into the liquid. Add the rest of the ingredients and blend until smooth. You may add extra coconut water or water if you desire a thinner consistency.

Food Substitution: Instead of apples, use mango, pineapple, berries of any variety, tangerines, kiwis or any other type of fruit. Substitute different green produce such as romaine lettuce, collard greens, parsley, cilantro or beet greens. Substitute ground flax seeds, hemp nut seeds or lecithin for chia seeds.

This recipe will make 1 quart. I recommend drinking it, over the morning by splitting it in half. Enjoy drinking it for breakfast and then as a mid-morning snack.

DAY ONE LUNCH
Cream of Asparagus Soup & Avocado Kale Salad

> Asparagus provides an excellent source of B vitamins including folic acid. B vitamins support and maintain energy levels. Folic acid is critical for healthy cell replication and DNA synthesis.

Cream of Asparagus Soup

1 bunch fresh Asparagus
2 Shallots, skins removed and ends trimmed
1 cup of warm purified water
3-4 T. Almond Butter, raw rounded
1 T. Olive Oil
1 Lemon, hand-juiced
1 clove Garlic
½ t. Herbamare seasoning salt
½ t. Sea Salt
1 t. Cumin, ground

Start: water warming on the stove. Only bring to point of medium steam and shut off heat. Separate the asparagus tips from the stems. Set the tips aside. Loosely chop the stems and place them in the food processor with the lemon juice and salt (*lemon juice combines with the salt to "cook" the asparagus making the nutrients more bio-available*). Puree. Add the almond butter, olive oil, garlic, Herbamare and cumin. Puree to smooth consistency. Slowly add warm water to thin the creamy soup base. Add the asparagus tips and the shallots to the food processor. Pulse-chop the asparagus tops and shallots into the creamy soup base. Serve directly out of food processor (into preheated warmed bowls, from the oven or warming drawer). You may gently heat the soup on the stove to 118 degrees before serving. This soup is delicious with unpasteurized cheese sprinkled on top. Serve & Enjoy!

Food Substitution: If asparagus is out of season, you may substitute with raw spinach. Use 4 cups of baby spinach, replace the almond butter with 1 avocado and replace cumin with 1 t. Garam Masala spice. Blend everything together, except warm water, which is slowly added last to reach desired soup consistency (you may add more or less warm water).

DAY ONE LUNCH
Cream of Asparagus Soup & Avocado Kale Salad

Avocado Kale Salad

1 head of Lacinata Kale aka. Dinosaur Kale, shredded
1 cup Cherry Tomatoes, diced
1 Avocado, chopped
3 T. Olive Oil
2 t. Lemon juice, to preferred taste
½-1 t. Sea Salt
¼-½ t. Cayenne Pepper

> Kale is rich in sulfur compounds. Sulfur has demonstrated an ability to stimulate detoxifying enzymes in the liver that neutralize carcinogens and prevent tumor growth.

Rinse: and clean kale. Place kale on a cutting board lengthwise. Hold firmly and roll tightly into a cigar-like shape. Chop off the bottom tough ends and discard. Start at the bottom and begin cutting thin strips until you have reached the top. Place the shredded kale into a large mixing bowl. Sprinkle with salt and stir well. Add the lemon juice and stir again making sure to evenly distribute the salt and lemon. Use your hands and massage the salt and lemon into the kale. This breaks down the cell wall of the kale making the nutrients more bio-available. Add the olive oil, avocado, tomatoes and cayenne pepper. Use your hands to massage and blend the rest of the ingredients into the salad. If massaging your salad does not appeal to you, you may choose to combine all of the ingredients together with a spoon or potato masher.

Serving Note: Live crackers with raw cheese on the side of this meal is delicious.

FOOD PREPARATION
DAY ONE DINNER - DAY TWO LUNCH

Food Preparation: Keep in mind you want be prepared in advance for mealtimes. This will help you be successful in completing the Gourmet Cleanse and will facilate a healthy nourshing lifestyle practice. To keep things easier for you I have written the menu plan so your dinner meal will also provide you with a delicious lunch. Keep this in mind and make allowances or adjustments for recipe amounts. Remember you do not have to go hungry while using the menu for this cleanse. The nutrients provided from this food are required for supporting the Phase 1 and Phase 2 biotransformation process so you can release damaging fat-soluable toxic substances and metabolic waste. Day 1 Dinner, soak ½ cup walnuts for 3-4 hours. You may substitute hemp nuts instead of walnuts as another option as they do not need to be soaked.

Day Two: Shopping List

Collard Greens, 1 bunch
Shiitake or Crimini Mushrooms, 1 cup combined
Kalamata Olives, ¼ cup
Capers, 2T.
Red Pepper, 1 medium size
Zucchini or Asparagus, 1 cup fresh
Sun-Dried Tomatoes, 1 jar (Mediterranean Organic, which
is marinated in Olive Oil and spices or 1 cup of sundried tomatoes)

Day 1 Dinner - Day 2 Lunch

Salad Extraordinaire
Sesame Miso Dressing

All vegetables are a source of D-glucarate which assists in converting fat-soluble xenobiotics into water-soluble compounds that can be excreted from the body. Beets are one of the best foods for building the blood due to their high non-heme iron content. They supply betaine which assists HCL production. Beets support and balance phase 1 & phase 2 Biotransformation processes.

DAY ONE DINNER
Salad Extraordinaire & Sesame Miso Dressing

Salad Extrordinare
4 cups Mixed Greens
3 Celery stalks
1 Bulb Fennel
1, 3-inch stalk Burdock Root
½ cup Cilantro, chopped
2 cups Spinach, chopped
¼ cup Arame seaweed, soaked 15 minutes, drained and rinsed
1 Avocado, peeled, pitted and chopped
½ cup Walnuts, soaked 3-4 hours,
drained and rinsed or 1/3 cup Hemp nuts (not soaked)
4 T. Feta Goat Cheese, optional
½ cup Red Onion, minced

> Spinach is an excellent source of magnesium, which is needed for glutathione production. This functions as the liver's main antioxidant.

Soak: arame seaweed for 15 minutes, drain and rinse well. Place mixed greens in salad bowl. Use the shredding blade on your food processor and alternate shredding 3 stalks celery, 1 bulb of fennel and burdock root. Add this layer on top of the mixed greens. Sprinkle your choice of nuts or seeds on top of the shredded vegetables. Use the S-Blade on the food processor to chop cilantro and spinach together. Layer this combo on top of the nuts. Layer the arame on top of the cilantro and spinach. Layer in the chopped avocado, cheese, and red onion. Dress with Sesame Miso Salad Dressing or, if you're short on time, use olive oil, apple cider vinegar, and fresh chopped herbs. Another dressing option is to use olive oil and Nama Shoyu.

Serving Note: Use this recipe to make enough salad for Day 2 lunch. Make sure to add the avocado, seaweed and Sesame Miso Dressing right before eating. Everything else can be made and stored in a covered container overnight.

DAY ONE DINNER
Salad Extraordinaire & Sesame Miso Dressing

Sesame Miso Salad Dressing

½ cup Olive Oil

¾ cup Water

2 T. Apple Cider Vinegar

3 T. Light Yellow Miso

6 T. Tahini, raw

1 Garlic, clove

3 T. Basil, fresh, or ½ t. dried

2 T. Oregano, fresh, or ½ t. dried

> Apple Cider Vinegar supports the digestive system by supplying additional enzymes & acids that break down food and increase nutrient assimilation.

Place: all ingredients into the blender and blend until smooth. This dressing has a tendency to thicken and may need additional water (2-3 T.) added, after it is stored in the refrigerator.

Sesame Miso salad dressing can be stored in the refrigerator and used for up to 10 days as the vinegar acts as a preservative. This dressing is delicious over wild rice and vegetables, quinoa or can be used as a veggie dip. These quick meal ideas can be substituted if you run short on time and are looking for something fast and easy. Make sure to include some leafy greens anytime you are enjoying the wild rice or quinoa with vegetables. Marinated collard greens stored in the refrigerator are always a good idea to have on hand to eat with wild rice or quinoa.

FOOD PREPARATION
DAY TWO DINNER - DAY THREE LUNCH

Food Preparation: Day 2 Dinner, soak 2 cups of wild rice in pure spring or filtered, warm water for 8-10 hours. This amount of rice will provide approximately 6 cups of soft chewable wild rice. Start by covering the wild rice in cold water (2 cups). The cold water protects the nutrients and enzymes in the wild rice. Add 2 cups warm steaming (not boiling) water. Add ¼ to ½ t. salt (this helps to "cook" the rice and adds minerals). Allow rice to soak in the jar, not refrigerated, in open air (no cover) for 8-10 hours. The rice will absorb the water, swell up and get tender. It is ok to soak longer than recommended time. After 8-10 hours the rice is ready to be drained, rinsed well, covered and stored in the refrigerator. Soaked and rinsed wild rice will last for 10 days in the refrigerator.

Marinate Collard Greens, place the greens on a cutting board lengthwise. Chop the tough uneven stems off the very bottom of the collard greens. Fold them in half (length-ways) and then roll them tightly, like a cigar. Use a sharp knife and cut them into thin strips. Put them into a bowl. Sprinkle them with ¼ t. salt and use your hands to massage the salt into the leaves. Add the juice of one lemon or lime, 6 basil leaves (chopped), 1 clove of garlic, 2 T. olive oil and a dash of cayenne pepper. Stir well so the collards are marinated. Cover and store in the refrigerator until dinner time tomorrow night.

On page 102 you will find the recipe for Quick Onion Crackers. If you have not prepared crackers yet, now is a good time to explore this recipe. If you are planning to have crackers with your soup for day 3 dinner you want to soak the sunflower seeds this evening. If you are in a hurry you may omit soaking the sunflower seeds, grind them dry and follow the recipe.

Day 2 Dinner - Day 3 Lunch

ITALIAN WILD RICE PILAF
MARINATED COLLARD GREENS

Shiitake Mushrooms have been used medicinally for over 6,000 years. Studies show one of the active ingredients is an immune strengthening compound called lentinan. Lentinan is a polysaccharide, beta-glucan which stimulates immune fighting reticular cells, known to ingest pathogenic bacteria.

DAY TWO DINNER
Italian Wild Rice Pilaf & Marinated Collard Greens

> Wild Rice is a grass that does not contain starch or gluten. Wild rice is flavorful and more nutritious than other forms of rice. It contains twice the amount of protein and iron as brown rice.

Italian Wild Rice Pilaf

4 cups Wild Rice, presoaked, drained and rinsed
1 cup Shiitaki or Crimini Mushrooms, remove tips off bottoms, wipe tops with damp paper towel
1 T. Olive Oil
1 T. Nama Shoyu, unpasteurized Soy Sauce
4 T. Basil, fresh or ½ t. of dried
3 T. Oregano, fresh or 1/3 t. dried
1 Garlic, clove
¼ cup Kalamata Olives
2 T. Capers
¼ cup Onions, diced
1 Red Pepper, medium-size, cleaned
1 cup Zucchini, Asparagus or other fresh vegetable of your choice
1 jar of Sun-Dried Tomatoes, marinated in Olive oil and fresh herbs (Mediterranean Organic brand or 1 cup sun-dried tomatoes)
1 t. Sea Salt

Step One: Steam 4 cups of pre-soaked wild rice for 5 minutes. After five minutes of steaming, shut off the heat, remove lid and give it a good stir (fluffing). Return lid, keep warm until you are ready to mix it into the vegetables.

DAY TWO DINNER
Italian Wild Rice Pilaf & Marinated Collard Greens

Step Two: Use the S-Blade of your food processor to pulse-chop mushrooms, being mindful to not over process. Place chopped mushrooms in a medium-size mixing bowl. Drizzle 1T. olive oil and 1T. Nama Shoyu sauce over the mushrooms and stir well. Pulse-chop raw garlic, basil and oregano. Stir herbs and garlic into mushrooms.

Pulse-chop, ¼ cup olives, stir in to mixture with capers. Pulse-chop onion, red pepper, and any other vegetables (zucchini or asparagus) and mix well. Add wild rice and salt to veggies. Pour olive oil from sun-dried tomatoes into the veggies/rice and stir well. Puree sun-dried tomatoes in food processor and then stir well, into your wild rice mixture. Adjust spices according to your taste.

> Fresh Extra Virgin Olive Oil provides healthy fat-soluble whole-food complex vitamins E, A, K, anti-inflammatory flavonoids, free-radical quenching antioxidants & anticoagulant polyphenols.

ServingNote: Spread Marinated Collard Greens on a plate. Place desired amount of Italian Rice Pilaf on top of the Marinated Collard Greens. Grate or crumble raw cheese on top of Wild Rice Pilaf. Enjoy with raw crackers.

Food Substitution: The variation on this recipe is endless so feel free to add other fresh veggies such as chopped broccoli, carrots, snow peas, English peas, chopped kale or spinach.

FOOD PREPARATION
DAY THREE DINNER - DAY FOUR LUNCH

Food Preparation: You will have 2 cups of wild rice left over (keep stored in refrigerator so you can add one cup to the Miso Soup for Day 3 Dinner. Other left over wild rice can be sprinkled into salads as desired.

Refer to the Quick Onion Cracker Recipe on page 102, if you want live crackers with your miso soup. You may purchase raw crackers or low-temperature baked sprouted Manna Bread from the freezer section at your local health food store. Manna Bread is sprouted and baked at a low temperature, however it contains gluten.

Day Three Shopping List

Shiitake Mushrooms, 2 cups
Zucchini, 1 medium
Red Pepper, 1 medium
Carrot, 1 large
Cilantro, ¾ cup
Cherry Tomato, 1 cup or 2 Roma, medium
Scallions, 4
Wakame Seaweed, 1 package
Wild Rice (Base Shopping List)
Olive Oil (Base Shopping List)
Nama Shoyu (Base Shopping List)
Miso Paste (Base Shopping List)
Almond Butter (Base Shopping List)
Garlic (Base Shopping List)

Day 3 Dinner - Day 4 Lunch

MISO VEGETABLE SOUP
QUICK ONION CRACKERS

Wakame Seaweed contains alginic acid which binds with toxic metallic elements in the intestines and is eliminated as waste. Wakame provides vitamin C and B-complex which includes B12. Wakame supplies alkaline minerals that cleanse the blood and tissues, while flushing impurities out of the lymph system.

DAY THREE DINNER
Miso Vegetable Soup & Quick Onion Crackers

Miso Vegetable Soup

2 cups Shiitake Mushrooms (cleaned by chopping off tips of bottoms and wiping with damp paper towel)
1 Zucchini
1 Red Pepper
1 large Carrot
¾ cup Cilantro
1 cup Cherry or 2 medium Roma Tomatos
4 Scallions, white bottoms only
2 t. dried Wakame Seaweed
1 cup soaked Wild Rice
3 T. Olive Oil
2 T. Nama Shoyu

> Red Pepper is a ripened green pepper. Red Pepper provides vitamin C and fat-soluble vitamins A & E complex. Olive oil increases fat-soluble vitamin absorption.

Step One: Steam one cup of wild rice for five minutes. Fluff, cover and keep it warm until ready to use.

Step Two: Pulse-chop mushrooms into ¼ pieces. Drizzle with 2T. of olive oil and 1T. soy sauce. Pulse-chop zucchini, stir into the mushrooms. Pulse-chop the red pepper, carrots, cilantro, tomatoes and scallions, individually. Take time to evenly stir them into the vegetable mixture after each ingredient. Crumble 2t. of dried wakame seaweed and stir it into the vegetable mixture. Add wild rice to the vegetables and mix well. Drizzle remaining 1T. olive oil and 1T. soy sauce into recipe and stir again well. Cover and allow mixture to marinate while you prepare the Miso Broth.

DAY THREE DINNER
Miso Vegetable Soup & Quick Onion Crackers

Miso Broth

6 cups warm purified water, approximately 120 degrees
4 T. Red Miso, measure rounded
4 T. Light Miso, measure rounded
3 T. raw Almond Butter, measure rounded
1-2 cloves Garlic

> Miso is a fermented soy paste that supplies whole B-complex vitamins and supports an environment for healthy symbotic bacteria to flourish.

Place: all ingredients in blender. Blend on high until you have a smooth consistency. Pour the miso broth into the vegetable mixture and stir everything together.

Serving Note: Warm your soup bowls in the oven prior to serving to keep the soup warm. Raw cheese and crackers make a wonderful addition to this delicious soup. You may heat this soup gently on the stove using a low temperature and stirring often. Another option is to eat this soup cold on a hot day.

FOOD PREPARATION
DAY FOUR DINNER - DAY FIVE LUNCH

Food Preparation: Soak 2 cups of quinoa in 4 cups of water. Begin by rinsing the quinoa really well in a colander to remove bitter taste. Place quinoa in a jar and put 2 cups cold water on top, to protect nutrients from warm water. Add 2 cups of steaming warm (not boiling) water. Allow it to sit on counter 8-10 hours uncovered. In the morning, drain off the soak water, rinse really well, store covered in the refrigerator.

Soak: ½ cup of sunflower seeds for eight hours. They will be added to the Quinoa Tabouli. You may dry them in the oven or dehydrator or you may choose to add them to the Tabouli wet. I prefer the crunchy version. Two other options: Instead of using sunflower seeds, replace them with pine nuts, which do not have to be soaked. Pine nuts are very soft and don't have many enzyme inhibitors to be removed. Another option is to use ¼ cup of hemp nut seeds, which do not have to be soaked. You can also use smaller amounts of two or all three of the nuts and seeds.

Day Four Shopping List

Parsley, ¾ cup
Red Onion, 1 or Scallions, 1 bunch
Cherry Tomatoes, 1 cup or 2 Roma Tomatoes, medium size
Sunflower Seeds, ½ cup or ¼ cup pine nuts, or ¼ cup Hemp Nut Seeds
Celery, 1 rib
Mint or Dill, fresh or dried
Green Olives, 8
Romaine Lettuce, 1 head

Day Four Dinner - Day Five Lunch

QUINOA TABOULI
& ROMAINE LETTUCE

Quinoa is an alkalizing ancient seed that contains all 8 essential amino acids which makes it a complete protein source. Quinoa is abundant in the amino acid lysine, which is easily destroyed by heat and manufacturing processes. Lysine is required in the production of many essential hormones which regulate body function and performance.

DAY FOUR DINNER
Quinoa Tabouli & Romaine Lettuce

> Low-temperature prepared Quinoa supplies an adequate amount of Lysine and Tryptophan. Lysine is used for healthy collagen, tissue growth & repair. Tryptophan regulates sleep patterns.

Quinoa Tabouli

5 cups Quinoa
¾ cup Parsley
¼ med. Red Onion or 6 Scallions (bottoms only)
2 Garlic, cloves
1 cup Cherry Tomatoes or 2 Roma (seeded/chopped)
½ cup Sunflower Seeds or ¼ pine nuts or ¼ cup hemp nut seeds (or combination)
1 Celery, rib
3 T. Olive Oil
¼ t. Sea Salt
2 T. Mint or Dill, fresh, 1t. dried)
8 Green Olives, chopped
8 Black Olives, chopped

Steam: quinoa for 7 minutes, remove lid and fluff with a spoon several times during the 7 minutes. Cover and keep warm. Use your food processor with the S-blade to chop the parsley and the garlic together. Put in a mixing bowl. Pulse-chop the black and green olives and add to the bowl. Pulse-chop the tomatoes and add to the bowl. Pulse-chop the celery and dill and/or mint together and add to the bowl. Pulse-chop the onions and add to the bowl. Stir in sea salt and mix everything together well. Add the steamed quinoa, seeds/nuts and stir again. Mix everything together, making sure it is evenly distributed. You may add a dash of squeezed lemon or lime juice if you like.

DAY FOUR DINNER
Quinoa Tabouli & Romaine Lettuce

Serving Note: Serve with chopped romaine lettuce on the side using the leftover Sesame Miso Dressing (from Day 1). Another delicious option is to stuff Quinoa Tabouli inside whole romaine lettuce leaves and use the Sesame Miso Dressing as a dipping sauce. Avocados, olives, cheese and raw crackers are a delicious addition.

> Parsley is rich in chlorophyll which oxygenates and cleanses the blood. It is beneficial for healthy blood flow as it dissolves blood clots and maintains elasticity in the blood vessels.

FOOD PREPARATION
DAY FIVE DINNER - DAY SIX LUNCH

Day 5 Shopping List

Arame Seaweed, ½ cup

Red Pepper, 1 large

Cucumber, med.-large size

Burdock Root, ½ Cup

Avocado, 1 ripe

Olive Oil (Base Shopping List)

Coconut Oil (Base Shopping List)

Sesame Oil, 1 jar, unroasted

Agave or raw unfiltered Honey (Base Shopping List)

Miso, light (Base Shopping List)

Nama Shoyu Sauce (Base Shopping List)

Tahini (Base Shopping List)

Garlic (Base Shopping List)

Ginger, 4-inch piece

Day Five Dinner - Day Six Lunch

Arame Salad
Ginger Tahini Miso Dressing
Mixed Greens & Avocado

Arame Seaweed is known in Japan to bring an abundance of health and wealth to all who eat it. Arame is normalizing to blood sugar levels and brings luster and resilience to hair. Arame expands four to five times in the stomach as it absorbs water so it is valuable as a weight reduction or maintenance aid. It supplies essential alkaline minerals for cleansing and vitamin A which protects lipid cellular membranes from damage. Vitamin A is essential for Phase 1 detoxification process.

DAY FIVE DINNER
Arame Salad with Ginger Tahini Miso Dressing

> Burdock Root is purifying to the body. Its actions include cleansing the liver and blood while simultaneously stimulating the metabolism and circulatory system. It is powerful anti-tumor agent.

Arame Salad

1 cup Arame Seaweed, soaked for 20 minutes in 1 cup of water, drained and rinsed
1 Red Pepper, large, julienne-sliced sticks
1 Cucumber, large and unpeeled, chopped into ¼-inch pieces
½ cup Burdock Root (no need to peel, just wash and scrub the outside)

Place: the soaked, drained and rinsed arame seaweed in a large bowl. Slice the red pepper into thin strips and stir into the seaweed. Pulse-chop the cucumber using the S-Blade of the food processor, taking care to not over process. Add cucumber and red pepper to the seaweed, stir. Pulse-chop the burdock root into small pieces and add to the salad. Mix everything together. The following Ginger Tahini Miso Dressing recipe will be used to dress the Arame Salad. This same recipe will be used as a dipping sauce for the Nori Rolls, so we will be making a double amount.

DAY FIVE DINNER
Arame Salad with Ginger Tahini Miso Dressing

Ginger Tahini Miso Dressing *or use as the Ginger Tahini Miso dipping sauce*

4 T. Olive Oil
2 T. Coconut Oil
4 T. Sesame Oil
4 T. Agave or Honey
2 T. Light Miso
6 T. Nama Shoyu
4 T. Tahini
2 clove Garlic
4 1-inch chunks of fresh peeled ginger

> Ginger is a rich source of phytonutrients known as gingerols. Gingerols are potent anti-inflammatory agents that reduce tissue swelling and inflammation. It also prevents nausea & vomiting.

Place: all ingredients in blender. Blend on high until you have a smooth consistency. Stir into the Arame Seaweed Salad.

Serving Note: Place mixed greens on plate. Chop some avocado and stir into the greens with a dash of olive oil and apple cider vinegar. Place Arame Seaweed Salad next to the mixed green salad and enjoy!

The salad dressing makes a double batch so make sure you save half of the dressing for a dipping sauce to be used for Nori Rolls, Day Six Dinner.

FOOD PREPARATION
DAY SIX DINNER - DAY SEVEN LUNCH

Food Preparation: For Day Six Dinner, soak 1 cup of sunflower seeds, 1 cup of pumpkin seeds and 1 cup of almonds for 8 hours. After eight hours drain off soak water, rinse and store, covered, in the refrigerator until you are ready to prepare dinner.

Day Six Shopping List

Nori Sheets, 1 package either toasted on not, your choice
Carrots, 2
Celery, 2 ribs
Zucchini, 1 medium
Sprouts, 1 cup either sunflower, broccoli or clover
Almonds, 1 cup
Red Pepper, 1 medium-large size
Raisins, ½ cup
Ginger Root, 2-inch piece
Sunflower Seeds (Base Shopping List)
Pumpkin Seeds (Base Shopping List)
Garlic (Base Shopping List)
Red Onion (Base Shopping List)
Nama Shoyu (Base Shopping List)

Day Six Dinner - Day Seven Lunch

Teriyaki Pate Nori Rolls
Ginger Tahini Miso Dipping Sauce

Nori Seaweed aides digestion and enhances the metabolism of fats which is balancing and promotes healthy cholesterol levels. Nori provides adequate amounts of B-vitamins for metabolizing carbohydrates for energy. It also contains vitamin A for repairing and protecting lipid membranes in the intestines for proper elimination. Nori contains vitamin C which performs as an antioxidant and sulfur-rich amino acids for supporting the phase 2 detoxification cycle in the liver.

DAY SIX DINNER
Teriyaki Pate Nori Rolls & Ginger Tahini Miso Dipping Sauce

> Sunflower Seeds are nutrient-rich in vitamin E which is essential for brain and heart health, protecting cholesterol from oxidizing and performs as an anti-inflammatory.

Teriyaki Pate

1 cup each: Sunflower Seeds, Pumpkin Seeds and Almonds
1 Red Pepper, cleaned
4 T. Olive Oil
1 clove Garlic
¼ cup Red Onion
2-inch cube Ginger Root, peeled
½ cup Raisins
¼ cup Nama Shoyu
½ cup purified Water

Step One: Begin soaking the raisins in the Nama Shoyu and water for thirty minutes.

Step Two: While the raisins are soaking place the pre-soaked nuts and seeds in the food processor and initiate blending. Add the rest of the ingredients including the raisins and their soaking liquid. Blend mixture together, making sure to leave some texture, however you do want to keep it some what creamy and smooth.

DAY SIX DINNER
Teriyaki Pate Nori Rolls & Ginger Tahini Miso Dipping Sauce

Teriyaki Pate Nori Rolls
1 Package Nori Sheets
1 Carrot
1 Celery Stalk
1 Zucchini, small
1 cup Sprouts, Sunflower, Broccoli or Clover

> Celery is low in calories, high in fiber and nutrition. It provides antioxidants known as flavonoids and coumarins which builds the immune system and destroys unhealthy cells. Great for balancing blood pressure.

Julienne-slice: (matchstick size) some carrots, celery, and zucchini. Put a bit of the pate on the Nori sheet, approximately 1 inch from the bottom. Now layer in some of the julienned veggies and sprouts. Roll tightly into a Nori Roll. You may use a bamboo rolling mat for the professional look. Wild rice can be sprinkled on top of the pate, before you roll.

Serving Note: Keep in mind that Nori rolls can get soggy, so if you are taking your lunch to go, carry your pate, veggies and Nori sheets separately and roll them up right before you eat. Serve with Ginger Tahini Dipping Sauce and Nama Shoyu. Other options for serving include cucumbers, red bell peppers and mixed greens, which are great compliments to this nutritious meal.

FOOD PREPARATION
DAY SEVEN DINNER - DAY EIGHT LUNCH

Day Seven: Shopping List

Red Peppers, 4
Cherry tomatoes, 1 cup
Cilantro, ¾ cup
Feta Cheese or raw cheese, optional
Bib Lettuce or another variety, 1 head
Avocado, ripe (Base Shopping List)
Red Onion (Base Shopping List)
Garlic (Base Shopping List)
Olive Oil (Base Shopping List)
Lime (Base Shopping List)
Almond Butter (Base Shopping List)
Lemon (Base Shopping List)
Herbamare (Base Shopping List)
Sea Salt (Base Shopping List)
Cumin (Base Shopping List)

Day Seven Dinner - Day Eight Lunch

Red Pepper Cilantro Soup
&
Bib Lettuce Rolls

Red peppers are ripened green peppers. They are a valuable source of vitamin C and A, as they contain numerous carotenoids including beta-carotene, alpha-carotene, beta-cryptoxanthin, lutein, lycopene and zeaxanthin. Carotenoids promote heart and vision health.

Cilantro is a delicious aromatic herb which cleanses the body with chlorophyll, removes heavy metals and provides an assortment of vitamins and minerals including B, C, E, A, K, calcium, magnesium, potassium, copper, iron and manganese.

DAY SEVEN DINNER
Red Pepper Cilantro Soup & Bib Lettuce Rolls with Feta Cheese

> Cumin has been used for over 5,000 years. It is plentiful in iron which builds strong blood, aids in proper enzyme function and manufacturing proteins. Cumin supports a healthy strong digestive system.

Red Pepper Cilantro Soup

4 Red Peppers, medium to large size
¾ cup Cilantro
1 Lime, hand juiced
4 T. Almond Butter, rounded, raw
1 T. Olive Oil
1 Garlic Clove, medium
½ t. Herbamare Seasoning Salt
½ t. Sea Salt
1t. Cumin, ground
¾ cup water, warmed to approximately 115 degrees

Step One: Gently warm water on the stove. Clean red peppers, remove stems and seeds. Place 1 of the red peppers in the food processor, with the S-Blade. Gently pulse-chop pepper into small, bite-size pieces, taking care to not over process. Set aside. Add the remaining 3 red peppers, cilantro, lime juice, almond butter, olive oil, garlic, seasoning and sea salt to the food processor. Blend to reach smooth consistency. While the processor is running, slowly add the warm water to thin, reaching desired soup base consistency. Stir in the bite-sized red pepper and serve. Options: You may add a dash of cayenne to spice it up a bit.

Serving Note: Gently warm on the stove and serve in pre-warmed soup bowls with raw crackers and feta cheese.

DAY SEVEN DINNER
Red Pepper Cilantro Soup & Bib Lettuce Rolls with Feta Cheese

Bib Lettuce Rolls

1 head Bib Lettuce, separate leaves and clean
1 Avocado, pit removed, scooped out and chopped into ¼-inch pieces
1 cup Cherry Tomatoes
¼ cup Cilantro
¼ cup Red Onion
1 Garlic, clove
Feta Cheese, crumbled
½ Lime
2 T. Olive Oil

> Onions prevent infections as they are one of nature's natural antibiotics. They contain allyl disulfate, an antiseptic oil and cycloallin an anticoagulant that prevents obstructions from accumulating on the walls of blood vessels.

Pulse-chop the tomato, red onion, cilantro and garlic. Place in a bowl. Stir in the avocado pieces. Hand-squeeze the lime juice over the mixture and add in the olive oil. Stir in the crumbled feta cheese. Put this mixture into the bib lettuce and roll into a wrap shape. You may substitute with romaine lettuce or red leaf lettuce if bib lettuce is unavailable.

FOOD PREPARATION
DAY EIGHT DINNER - DAY NINE LUNCH

Food Preparation: Day Eight Dinner, soak 2 cups of raw pumpkin seeds in purified water for 8 hours. You can do this overnight. After 8 hours, drain, rinse, cover and store in container until you are ready to make the Jalapeño Pumpkin Seed Pate.

Day Eight: Shopping List

Red Pepper, 1
Japapeno Pepper, 1
Cilantro, 1 ½ cups
Parsley, ¼ cup
Beet Green Tops, 1 bunch
Tomatoes, 3 cups Cherry or 3 Roma
Avocados, 2 or more
Plain Yogurt (goat, raw is best)
Garlic (Base Shopping List)
Red Onion (Base Shopping List)
Lime (Base Shopping List)
Apple Cider Vinegar (Base Shopping List)
Sea Salt (Base Shopping List)
Pumpkin seeds, 2 cups (Base Shopping List)

Day Eight Dinner - Day Nine Lunch

Jalapeño Pumpkin Beet Green Enchiladas
Guacamole & Salsa

Pumpkin Seeds are one of the best sources of nutrition for the male prostrate gland as well as the female endocrine system, due to high levels of zinc, magnesium and omega-3 fatty acids. Studies show magnesium and zinc are the two minerals most people have a deficiency in. Pumpkin seeds contain myosin, which is the main protein compound of muscle tissue essential for muscular contraction.

Beet Greens are tender and delicious when eaten in their raw state. They are plentiful in phytonutrients that dissolve and cleanse acidic waste build-up in the kidneys, intestines, lymph, liver and gallbladder. Beet greens are a source of oxalic acid, which increases the movement of fluids when consumed raw. When beet greens and other greens such as spinach are cooked the oxalic acid binds with minerals such as calcium and magnesium, preventing absorption.

DAY EIGHT DINNER
Jalapeño Pumpkin Beet Green Enchiladas Guacamole Salsa & Raw Crackers

> Jalapeño peppers help boost the circulatory system, normalize blood pressure, increase saliva & stomach acid production & promote peristaltic movement which aides in elimination.

Jalapeño Pumpkin Pate

2 cups Pumpkin Seeds, soaked, drained and rinsed
½ Red Pepper
½ Lime, juiced
1 clove Garlic
1 cup Cilantro
¼ cup Parsley
1 T. Coconut Oil
¼ cup Olive Oil
½-1 Jalapeño, cleaned and seeded
2 T. Plain Yogurt, served on top each enchilada
1 bunch of Beet Green Tops

Separate: beet tops from bottoms, leaving the long red red stems attached. Clean beet greens and set roots aside. Place pumpkin seeds, red pepper, lime juice, garlic, cilantro, parsley, coconut oil, olive oil, and jalapeño into the food processor utilizing the S-Blade. Blend until smooth. Stuff 2-3 T. Jalapeño Pumpkin Pate into each individual beet green. The amount of pate used depends on the size of the beet green.

Serving Note: Once you have the Beet Green Enchiladas assembled, place 2-3 of the enchiladas on a plate. Drizzle plain yogurt over the top of the Beet Green Enchiladas. Add some mixed greens or chopped romaine lettuce on the side. Grate some of the beets you previously set aside and add to the salad. Serve with Salsa, Guacamole, chopped olives and crackers.

DAY EIGHT DINNER
Jalapeño Pumpkin Beet Green Enchiladas Guacamole Salsa & Raw Crackers

Fresh Salsa

3 cups Ripe Roma Tomatoes or Cherry Tomatoes
½ cup Cilantro
2 T. Garlic
2 T. Red Onion
½ Serrano or Jalapeño Pepper, cleaned and seeded
1 ½ T. Lime juice
1 ½ T. Apple Cider Vinegar
1 t. Sea Salt

> Tomatoes are 93% water and produce a potent alkalizing effect, as they stimulate liver function in filtering and cleansing. Raw tomato is beneficial for liver inflammation & appendicitis.

Chop: enough cilantro, garlic, and red onion for both the Salsa and Guacamole recipes. Make the Salsa recipe first. Set aside the cilantro, garlic and red onion for the Guacamole. Add the tomatoes, spicy pepper, lime juice and apple cider vinegar. Gently Pulse-chop, leaving chunks for salsa texture.

Food Substitution: If you can't find quality Beet Greens, another option would be to use collard greens or romaine lettuce, however beet greens are tender, delicious and loaded with nutrients.

DAY EIGHT DINNER
Jalapeño Pumpkin Beet Green Enchiladas Guacamole Salsa & Raw Crackers

> Avocado is one of nature's most perfect foods as the Ph is close to perfect balance, it is nutrient-dense in essential vitamins, amino-acids, fatty acids and minerals that regulate body growth and function.

Guacamole
2 Avocados, ripe and fresh
1 Clove Garlic, chopped
1 T. Red Onion, chopped
2 T. Lime or Lemon juice
¼ cup Cilantro, chopped
½ t. Sea Salt

Cut: avocado in half, remove seed, and set the seed aside. Scoop out fruit with a spoon into a bowl. Sprinkle with salt and hand-squeeze the citrus juice over the avocado. Use a fork to mash the avocado, leaving some small chunks for consistency. Stir in the chopped red onion, cilantro and garlic. Add the avocado pit to the center of the Guacamole to prevent oxidation, cover tightly until you are ready to serve and store in the refrigerator. Guacamole will not store overnight as the oils will go rancid and it will turn brown.

Food Preparation: The key to awesome Guacamole is fresh, ripe avocados. You want them to have just turned soft, however there is no space between the peel and the inside fruit. If you cut an avocado and see brown spots and strings, don't consume. The oils in avocado can go rancid very quickly, which is unhealthy to eat and can make you sick.

NOTES

FOOD PREPARATION
DAY NINE DINNER - DAY TEN LUNCH

Food Preparation: Day Nine Dinner, soak 2 cups of wild rice using the method described on page 42 (end of Day One, Food Preparation note). Drain, rinse well and store in tightly covered container after 8-10 hours of soaking, draining and rinsing.

Day Nine: Shopping List

Basil, ½ cup, fresh
Green Onions, 2
Celery Ribs, 2
Kalamata Olives, 10 pitted, or ¼ cup Olive Tapanade
Grape Leaves, 1 jar or Collard Greens, Romaine Lettuce, 1 bunch
Garlic (Base Shopping List)
Pumpkin Seeds, 2 cups (Base Shopping List)
Avocado, 3 (note you will be needing Avocado's over the next few days, Base Shopping List)

Day Nine Dinner - Day Ten Lunch

Stuffed Grape Leaves
Greek Salad
with
Fresh Dill Dijon

Grape leaves provide vitamin C, A and E-complex, vitamin K, B2, B3, B6, folic acid, fiber, calcium, magnesium, copper, iron and manganese.

Wild rice is an excellent source of B vitamins which promotes metabolic energy, relieves stress, enhances mental clarity and is a rich source of soluble fiber which aides the elimination system.

DAY NINE DINNER
Stuffed Grape Leaves & Greek Salad with Fresh Dill Dijon

> Basil has a rich spicy taste which stimulates the appetite & stomach, aiding in digestive strength and the ability to assimilate nutrients. Basil is beneficial for nausea, flatulence and dysentery as it supports warming systemic balance.

Stuffed Grape Leaves

2 cups Wild Rice, soaked, drained and rinsed

½ cup Basil, fresh

1 Avocado

2 Green Onions, white bottoms only, trimmed

2 Celery Stalks

10 Kalamata Olives, pitted or ¼ cup Olive Tapanade

1 Garlic, clove

1 jar Grape Leaves or 1 Bunch Romaine Lettuce or Collard Greens

Remove: the grape leaves from jar, gently unwind and separate them. Rinse very well to remove salt brine from the leaves. Set individually aside to dry. Place wild rice in food processor. Process for several minutes for finer texture. Add the basil, green onions, celery and garlic. Process again for several minutes. Stop and scrape down the sides. Add the olives and avocado and process again, mixing in all of the ingredients. Pause, scrape down the sides and blend again until smooth.

Use two grape leaves to make one stuffed grape leaf roll. Lay out the grape leaves, end to end (there are small nodules at the base of the leaf which is the end). Slide the ends towards each other, until each end is in the middle of the other leaf, so they are over-lapping each other. Place 2 T. of the wild rice mixture approximately 1/3 of the way up from the bottom leaf. Begin to roll the grape leaf up from the bottom, tucking the ends into the roll as you go. Place the Stuffed Grape Leaves into an airtight container as you make them. Once you have completed the process, serve them or store them, tightly covered in the refrigerator for up to 5 days.

DAY NINE DINNER
Stuffed Grape Leaves & Greek Salad with Fresh Dill Dijon

Greek Salad with Fresh Dill Dijon

1 head of Spinach, Romaine or Red Leaf Lettuce, or combination

1½ cups Cherry Tomatoes, cut

1 Cucumber, medium sized, chopped into ¼-inch pieces

1/3 cup Kalamata Olives, chopped

¼ cup Feta Cheese, crumbled

¼ cup Red Onion, chopped

1 cup Broccoli Sprouts

> Dill is a rich source of antioxidants and volatile oils that prevent bacterial overgrowth. Dill contains numerous flavonoids that balance detox pathways and activates glutathione, which destroys free-radical scavengers.

Clean: Clean greens and place in large salad bowl. Add the chopped cherry tomatoes, cucumbers, kalamata olives, red onion and feta cheese. Toss with Fresh Dill Dijon dressing and garnish with broccoli sprouts.

Serving tip: You may substitute collard greens or romaine lettuce for the grape leaves or serve on the side of the Greek Salad, as a pate.

DAY NINE DINNER
Stuffed Grape Leaves & Greek Salad with Fresh Dill Dijon

> Tahini is a creamy spread made from hulled, ground sesame seeds. It is easily digested, contains 45% protein, 55% oil and provides a rich source of vitamin E & calcium. Excellent for bone and teeth health.

Fresh Dill Dijon

4 T. Mustard, prepared
2 T. Nama Shoyu
½ t. Himalayan Crystal Salt
¼ cup Apple Cider Vinegar
1 T. Tahini, raw
1 T. Olive Oil
1 T. Coconut Oil
1 T. Lemon Juice
4 sprigs of Dill, roughly chopped
1 T. raw Honey or Agave
¼ cup Water, purified

Blend: all ingredients until smooth.

Food Preparation: Make sure to save some of the Greek Salad for tomorrow's lunch. Cover and store it in the refrigerator without the dressing or cut tomatoes, so it doesn't get soggy.

Food Substitution: An option to making the Fresh Dill Dijon salad dressing is to toss the salad with ¼ cup olive oil, 4 sprigs of fresh dill (chopped) and ¼ cup apple cider vinegar.

NOTES

FOOD PREPARATION
DAY TEN DINNER - DAY ELEVEN LUNCH

Food Preparation: Day Ten, No Food Preparation Today

Day Ten: Shopping List

Pine Nuts, 1 cup
Basil, fresh 1 cup
Spinach, 1 cup
Zucchini, 4 medium-size
Romaine Lettuce, 1 head
Celery, 1 large rib
Kelp, 1½ T. powdered
Medjool Dates, 3
White Miso, 2 T. or Dijon Mustard, 1 T.
Lemon Juice, 4 T. (Base Shopping List)
Sea Salt (Base Shopping List)
Olive Oil, 1 cup total (Base Shopping List)
Garlic, 1-2 cloves (Base Shopping List)
Nama Shoyu (Base Shopping List)

Day Ten Dinner - Day Eleven Lunch

Zucchini Noodles with Pesto Sauce & Cesar Salad

Garlic is nature's natural antibiotic. Garlic is recognized as one of the most beneficial foods for digestive health and has a strong cleansing action on the lymph system as it promotes the elimination of noxious waste matter. Garlic is effective at removing lead and other toxic heavy metals from the body. It is known as an antifungal, antibacterial, antiseptic, antiviral, carminative and expectorant. Garlic cleanses the alimentary canal of unwanted guests, purifies the blood by dissolving inorganic deposits, boosts the immune system and regulates liver and gallbladder function.

DAY TEN DINNER
Zucchini Noodles with Pesto Sauce & Ceasar Salad

> Pine Nuts provide a very rich source of protein and fat, so small amounts are required before satiation is felt. Pine nuts are a source of magnesium, phosphorus, potassium, calcium, iron and zinc, B1, B2, B3 & fat-soluble vitamin A.

Zucchini Noodles with Pesto Sauce

1 cup pine nuts

3 cups Basil, fresh

1/3 cup Olive Oil

1 cup Spinach

1 t. Sea salt

1 Garlic Clove, large

4 zucchini

Use: a potato peeler and make long fettuccini-noodle-like strips out of the zucchini. The other option is to use a spiral vegetable cutter and make thin spaghetti noodles out of the zucchini. The spiral vegetable cutter is called a spiral slicer or spiralizer.

Combine all remaining ingredients and blend to smooth consistency. Stir into zucchini noodles. You may lightly heat the zucchini in some olive oil prior to adding the pesto sauce to soften and warm the squash, however it is delicious raw.

Serving Note: You may serve this recipe on top of mixed greens, arugula, baby spinach or stuffed inside radicchio, romaine lettuce or Chinese cabbage leaves.

DAY TEN DINNER
Zucchini Noodles with Pesto Sauce & Ceasar Salad

Ceasar Salad

1 head of Romaine, cleaned, chopped and set aside in salad bowl
½ cup Olive Oil
1-2 Garlic, cloves
Celery, 1 large rib
1½ T. White Miso or 1 T. prepared Dijon Mustard
4 T. Lemon Juice
½ cup Water
1 T. Nama Shoyu
1 t. Sea Salt
1 ½ T. Kelp
3 Medjool Dates, pitted

> Mustard Seeds belong to the brassicas family. They contain phytonutrients which inhibit tumors from forming. They provide, selenium, which prevents cancer & magnesium which promotes rest and relaxation, aiding in digestion.

Place: all ingredients, except romaine lettuce, into blender and blend until smooth. Dress the salad and serve immediately. Remember to only dress the salad you plan to eat right away. Cover and store the remaining dressing in the refrigerator for up to 5 days.

FOOD PREPARATION
DAY ELEVEN DINNER - DAY TWELVE LUNCH

Food Preparation: Chop 1 cup shiitake mushrooms, ½ cup cilantro, ½ cup basil and ¼ cup red onion. Place in storage container or jar with a lid. Hand-squeeze ½ lemon over vegetables and herbs. Drizzle in olive oil and stir well, mixing in the lemon juice and olive oil. Store in refrigerator and allow vegetables to marinate until tomorrow night. You may have some wild rice left over from Day Nine. If not, you'll need to soak 2 cups of the Wild Rice or you may choose to serve the Thai Stir Fry over quinoa, which will also need to be soaked prior to Day Eleven Dinner.

Day Eleven: Shopping List

Shiitake Mushrooms, 1 cup
Red Cabbage, 1 cup
Chinese Cabbage, 1 cup
Red Pepper, 1 medium-large
Ginger, 2-inch piece
Orange, 1 juiced
Cilantro, ½ cup
Basil, ½ cup
Cherry Tomatoes or vine-ripened Tomatoes, 1 cup
Snow Peas, ½ cup
Red Onion or Shallots, ¼ cut (Base Shopping List)
Avocado, perfectly ripe (Base Shopping List)
Olive Oil (Base Shopping List)
Light Miso (Base Shopping List)
Lemon Zest (Base Shopping List)
Garlic (Base Shopping List)
Nama Shoyu (Base Shopping List)
Sea Salt (Base Shopping List)

Day Eleven Dinner - Day Twelve Lunch

Thai Stir-Fry Over Wild Rice

Red Cabbage is a member of the cruciferous family of vegetables that contributes to building a healthy body. These benefits include a sweeping and cleansing action of putrefactive waste from the stomach and bowels, supplying essential nutrients which aid in alkalizing the body, stimulating the immune system, killing bacteria and viruses, preventing cancer cells from forming and clearing the complexion. Cabbage is an excellent source of vitamin C which functions as an antioxidant in Phase Two detoxification pathway.

DAY ELEVEN DINNER
Thai Stir-Fry Over Wild Rice

> Snow Peas are nourishing to the stomach, liver, spleen and pancreas because of their delicious sweet taste. They supply calcium, magnesium potassium, iron and phosphorus, with fiber which balances blood sugar levels.

Thai Stir Fry

1 cup Shiitake Mushrooms
1 cup Red Cabbage, shredded
1 cup Chinese Cabbage, shredded
1 Red Pepper, medium-large size
½ cup Cilantro
½ cup Basil
1 cup Cherry Tomatoes or vine-ripened Tomatoes, chopped
½ cup Snow Peas
¼ cup Red Onion or Shallots
1 Avocado, ripe and hand-chopped into ¼-inch pieces

Step One: Shred 1 cup of Chinese cabbage and one cup of red cabbage. Place in mixing bowl. Pulse-chop red peppers, snow peas and tomatoes. Be careful not to over process. Add to the bowl. Stir in the marinated mushrooms and herbs you prepared earlier, along with the chopped avocado and mix everything together well.

DAY ELEVEN DINNER
Thai Stir-Fry Over Wild Rice

Thai Stir Fry Sauce

½ cup Olive Oil
¼ cup Orange Juice
1 T. Light Miso
1 t. Lemon Zest (peel grated)
1 Garlic clove
1, 2-inch piece Ginger, peeled
3 T. Nama Shoyu
½ t. Sea Salt

> Lemon is the most alkalizing of all fruits. It contains essential nutrients that cleanse the blood & tissues of acids. Lemon stimulates the liver and gallbladder due to limonene, which also balances Phase 1 & 2 Detoxification pathways.

Steam: the wild rice (or quinoa) for five minutes. Place all recipe items into the food processor. Blend thoroughly. Pour sauce over vegetables in the mixing bowl and mix together completely.

Serving Note: Place 1½ cups of the wild rice on a pre-warmed plate and gently spoon 1 cup of the stir-fry vegetables with sauce on top of the wild rice. You may warm this dish in your oven on a low temperature for a few minutes, in your dehydrator for up to 2 hours (allowing the flavors to blend) or eat it cold. Any way you choose is delicious!

FOOD PREPARATION
DAY TWELVE DINNER - DAY THIRTEEN LUNCH

Food Preparation: Soak 1 cup of raw cashews for 6-8 hours, drain and rinse well.

Day Eleven: Shopping List

Zucchini, medium size, peeled, 2
Cashews, soaked, drained and rinsed, ½ cup
raw Tahini, ¾ cup
Olive oil, ¼ cup
Garlic cloves, 2
Sea Salt 1½ t.
Cumin, ground, 1t.
Coriander, ¼ t.
Jalapeño, 1
Romaine Lettuce, 1 head or Collard Greens
Tomatoes, 3 cups Cherry or Roma
Cilantro, ½ cup
Lemon, 1
Lime, 2
Coriander
Cumin (Base Shopping List)
Apple Cider Vinegar (Base Shopping List)
Garlic (Base Shopping List)
Red Onion (Base Shopping List)
Sea Salt (Base Shopping List)

Day Twelve Dinner - Day Thirteen Lunch

Mexi-Hummus
Fresh Salsa & Guacamole

Zucchini is available all year around. It provides a generous source of vitamin C and lutein, which supports eye health. Vitamin C prevents diseases such as asthma and scurvy. It also reduces skin damage and bruising. Zucchini is high in water and fiber content and low in calories so it is a perfect diet food. It has been shown to reduce homocysteine levels, a well-known cause of coronary heart disease and prevents colon cancer.

DAY TWELVE DINNER
Mexi-Hummus, Fresh Salsa & Guacamole

> Romaine Lettuce is a rich source of vitamin E which functions like a "lightening rod". It protects the cellular membrane from damage when free radicals strike. It supplies chromium stabalizing blood sugar levels.

Mexi-Hummus

2 Zucchini, medium size, peeled
½ cup Cashews, soaked, drained and rinsed
¾ cup raw Tahini
3 T. Lime or Lemon juice
¼ cup Olive oil
2 Garlic cloves, small or 1 medium
1½ t. Sea Salt
1t. Cumin, ground
¼ t. Coriander
¼ cup Parsley

Place: all ingredients into the food processor and blend until smooth. Open the romaine or collard green leaf and stuff with the hummus. Top with fresh Guacamole (recipe on page 70) and Fresh Salsa (recipe on page 69).

Food Preparation: The key to awesome Guacamole is fresh, ripe avocados. You want them to have just turned soft, however there is no space between the peel and the inside fruit. If you cut an avocado and see brown spots and strings, throw it away or return it to the store. The oils in avocado can go rancid very quickly, which is unhealthy to consume and can make you sick.

Serving Note: You may sprinkle 5-minute steamed quinoa or wild rice into the wrap. Garnish with plain yogurt, chopped cilantro, sprouts of your choice and raw cheese. Raw crackers are delicious with this meal.

NOTES

FOOD PREPARATION
DAY THIRTEEN DINNER - DAY FORTEEN LUNCH

Food Preparation: Day Thirteen Dinner, make sure to soak either 3 cups of quinoa or wild rice, unless you are planning to have the Marinara Sauce over spiralized zucchini noodles.

Day Thirteen: Shopping List

Cherry Tomatoes, 1 basket or 3 Roma Tomatoes
Sun-dried Tomatoes, 1 jar marinated in Olive Oil
Carrots, ½ cup
Currants 3 T.
Wild Rice, Quinoa or Zucchini noodles (your choice)
Spinach, one head or 6 cups baby spinach
Kalamata Olives, 10
Mint, 4 T. fresh
Feta Cheese or other raw cheese
Oregano, 4 T., fresh, 2 T. dried
Basil 6 T., fresh, 4 T. dried
Rosemary 2 T., fresh, 1 T. dried
Nama Shoyu (Base Shopping List)
Garlic (Base Shopping List)
Red Onion (Base Shopping List)
Apple Cider Vinegar (Base Shopping List)
Olive Oil (Base Shopping List)

Day Thirteen Dinner - Day Fourteen Lunch

Marinara Sauce
Zucchini Noodles
Wilted Spinach Salad

Marinara Sauce over Zucchini Noodles served with Wilted Spinach Salad is highly alkalizing and prevents systemic acidosis from occurring. The phytonutrient compounds in zucchini support various liver functions including cleansing the blood, metabolizing and utilizing carbohydrates, fats, proteins and hormones. Zucchini contains ample amounts of carotenoids that act as fat-soluble antioxidants.

Tomatoes are a valuable source of lycopene which studies show, prevent various cancers including prostate, stomach and lung cancer. Most of the nutrients are found in the skin and gel-like substance surrounding the seeds. Avoid eating unripe green tomatoes as they contain a toxin known as solanine and produce undesirable acid waste.

DAY THIRTEEN DINNER
Marinara Sauce over Zucchini Noodles with Wilted Spinach Salad

> Carrots are one of the most nutritious foods for the liver and digestive system. They balance the endocrine system, support kidney health and provide soluble pectin fiber for sweeping the colon clean.

Marinara Sauce

2 cups Cherry Tomatoes or three ripe Roma Tomatoes
1 cup of Sun-dried Tomatoes, marinated in Olive Oil
½ cup Carrots
3 T. Olive Oil, from Sun-dried Tomatoes
4 T. Oregano, fresh or 2 T. dried
6 T. Basil, fresh or 4 T. dried
2 T. Rosemary, fresh 1 T. dried
1 T. Nama Shoyu
2 T. Currants
2 Garlic, cloves
½ t. Sea Salt
Wild Rice, Quinoa or Zucchini noodles (your choice)

Place: all ingredients, except the zucchini into the food processor, with the S-Blade and blend until desired consistency. You want the sauce to have a smooth texture and be well blended. Use a potato peeler or a spiralizer to create the zucchini noodles. Pour Marinara Sauce over the top of the noodles. Garnish with shredded raw cheese.

Serving Note: You may gently warm the zucchini noodles with a light steam or pre-warmed olive oil in a skillet. Another option is to serve the marinara sauce over wild rice or quinoa.

DAY THIRTEEN DINNER
Marinara Sauce over Zucchini Noodles with Wilted Spinach Salad

Wilted Spinach Salad

1 head Spinach, 6 cups baby Spinach or one head, cleaned
10 Kalamata Olives, chopped
4 T. Mint, fresh, finely chopped
¼ cup Red Onion, finely chopped
Feta Cheese, crumbled
2 T. Apple Cider Vinegar
6 T. Olive Oil, gently warmed on stove top

> High Quality Sea Salt contains the 84 elements found in the human body which helps to regulate fluids, stabilizes blood sugar & sleep patterns, strengthens bone density, balances pH & blood pressure & supports libido.

Place: spinach in a salad bowl. Add all of the ingredients except the olive oil and vinegar. Toss thoroughly. Add the apple cider vinegar and toss again. Gently heat the oil on the stove. If the oil heats to a smoking temperature, throw it away and start again. Drizzle the warm oil over the salad and serve.

FOOD PREPARATION
DAY FOURTEEN DINNER

Food Preparation: Day Fourteen dinner make sure you have 4 cups of pre-soaked wild rice. Soak ½ cup Pecans for 4-8 hours, drain, rinse and store until ready to use.

Day Fourteen: Shopping List

Shiitake Mushrooms, 1 cup
Crimini mushrooms, 3 cups
Celery, ¾ cup
Shallot, 1 small
Zucchini, 1 small
Onion, 1/3 cup yellow
Black Pepper, ½ t.
Parsley, 4 T. fresh
Thyme, 2 T. fresh, 1 t. dried
Sage, 2 T. fresh, 1 t. dried
Pecans, ½ cup
Cauliflower, 1 head
Thyme, 2 T. fresh, 1 t. dried
Garlic (Base Shopping List)
Lemon (Base Shopping List)
Cashews (Base Shopping List)
Nama Shoyu (Base Shopping List)
Sea Salt (Base Shopping List)
Olive Oil (Base Shopping List)
Sea Salt (Base Shopping List)
Wild Rice, 4 cups (Base Shopping List)
Almond Butter, 4 T. raw (Base Shopping List)
Dark Red Miso 1 T. (Base Shopping List)

Day Fourteen Dinner

Savory Herb Wild Rice
Whipped Cauliflower
Mushroom Gravy
Extraodinaire

Cauliflower is a member of the brassica genus family or cabbage family. These various types of vegetables contain powerful anti-cancer substances known as indoles and dithiolthiones. Cauliflower provides the trace element boron, which is important for the absorption of magnesium and calcium. Magnesium is critical for glutathione production and is responsible for activating numerous detoxifying enzymes used in the biotransformation process.

DAY FOURTEEN DINNER
Savory Herb Wild Rice, Whipped Cauliflower & Mushroom Gravy Extraordinaire

Savory Herb Wild Rice

4 cups Wild Rice, soaked, drained, rinsed and 5-minute-steamed
1 cup Crimini Mushrooms
½ cup Shiitake Mushrooms
4 T. Nama Shoyu
4 T. Olive Oil
¾ cup Celery
1 Shallot, small
1 t. Sea Salt
½ t. Black Pepper
2 T. Parsley, fresh, chopped
2 T. Thyme, fresh or 1 t. dried
2 T. Sage, fresh or 1 t. dried
½ cup Pecans, soaked, drained, rinsed

> Sage contains antioxidant enzymes, volatile oils and phenolic acids. This powerful combination stabilizes oxygen and fat related metabolism, preventing several types of free radical tissue damage.

Place: mushrooms into food processor and pulse-chop to ¼-inch pieces. Put in mixing bowl and drizzle with 2 T. Nama Shoyu and 2 T. olive oil. Stir well. Pulse-chop all of the fresh herbs together, including parsley, thyme and sage. If you are using dried herbs just stir them into the mushrooms. Pulse-chop celery, shallot and pecans into ¼-inch pieces. Stir them in well. Add wild rice, salt, remaining olive oil and Nama Shoyu. Taste and adjust the spices if necessary.

DAY FOURTEEN DINNER
Savory Herb Wild Rice, Whipped Cauliflower & Mushroom Gravy Extraordinaire

Whipped Cauliflower

1 head of Cauliflower, light 5-minute steam
1 Garlic Clove, small
¼ cup Pinenuts
¼ cup Cashews, raw
1 Zucchini, small
2 T. Olive Oil
1 T. Namy Shoyu
2 T. Parsley, fresh
½ t. Sea Salt

> Cashews provide Oleic fatty-acids also found in olive oil. This type of oil has shown to reduce triglyceride levels which are fats carried in the blood. High levels of triglycerides have been associated with CVD.

Peel: zucchini making sure to remove all green from the outside. Pulse-chop the peel and add it to your Savory Herb Wild Rice. Place peeled zucchini and all remaning ingredients into the food processor and blend until smooth. You may serve them as they come out of the food processor or transfer the mixture into a pan to warm them gently, to approximately 118 degrees.

Serving Note: If you don't like mushrooms you can make a quick easy gravy recipe. Just blend 1 cup of water with 2 T. unpasteurized miso, 2 T. raw almond butter, a pinch of black pepper and any other herbs (fresh or dried) you like.

DAY FOURTEEN DINNER
Savory Herb Wild Rice, Whipped Cauliflower & Mushroom Gravy Extraordinaire

> Crimini Mushrooms provide selenium which is required to manufacture glutathione & copper, imperative for manufacturing SOD, two essential antioxidants. Crimini mushrooms are an excellent source of B-vitamin complex.

Mushroom Gravy Extraordinaire

½ cup Purified Water, warmed to approximately 118 degrees
4 T. Shiitake Mushrooms
2 T. Olive Oil
2 cups Crimini Mushrooms
4 T. raw Almond Butter, rounded
1 T. Dark Red Miso
1 T. Nama Shoyu
¼ t. Sea Salt
1 Garlic Clove, small

Pulse-chop: shiitake mushrooms into ¼-pieces. Transfer to a small warming pan. Drizzle Nama Shoyu and olive oil over the mushrooms and marinate for fifteen minutes. Put warm water, garlic, miso, almond butter, crimini mushrooms and salt into the food processor and blend well. Stir into the shiitake mushrooms in the warming pan then heat to approximately 118 degrees.

Serving Note: Place wild rice and whipped cauliflower onto a pre-warmed plate. Smother with Mushroom Gravy Extrordinaire. Enjoy!

CONGRATULATIONS!

Congratulations! You have successfully completed The Power of Chow, 14-Day Gourmet Cleanse & Rejuvenation Program. Give yourself a "Giant Hug" and a big pat on the back for taking the initiative to support your body in cleansing, healing and repairing! I hope you have learned a lot about yourself along with new nutritional information and recipes that will further your health and vitality. I sincerely appreciate each and every one of you and your commitment to following through. Thanks for your participation!

Live Well and Be Well,
Eloise

NOTES

MORE RECIPES

Quick Onion Flatbread Crackers & Herbal Flax Crackers

Crackers

You may want to make some live crackers prior to the beginning of The Gourmet Cleanse. Raw crackers are delicious and easy to make. They replace the craving for eating starchy processed snacks and are loaded with healthy seeds, nuts and vegetables. I always make a double batch because they store well in the refrigerator and will last up to 6 months. They are a great addition to meal-time and provide a component to a filling snack. Great for kids of all ages too.

Quick Onion Flatbread Crackers

1½ cups Sesame Seeds, hulled
1½ cups Flax Seeds
2 cups Sunflower Seeds (soaked=longer drying time, unsoaked=shorter drying time)
6 Green Scallions, large or 10 small, white bottoms only
1 Zucchini, small or medium, the larger the zucchini the softer the bread
¼ cup Nama Shoyu
½ cup Olive Oil
1 t. Sea Salt

> Sesame Seeds contain a unique compound known as sesamin which balances cholesterol levels and inhibits the absorption of old cholesterol. A nutrient-rich source of vitamin E which strengthens the nervous system.

Place: scallions and zucchini in foods processor. Blend. Separately grind the sesame seeds, flax seeds and dry sunflower seeds in your coffee grinder. If you soaked the sunflower seeds add those directly into the food processor. Put remaining ground seeds into the food processor with scallions, zucchini and other ingredients. Blend until smooth. Lay out on dehydrator teflex sheet approximately ¼-inch thick. Dry for 8 hours. Flip onto a screen sheet and dry for 8 more hours. You may also low-temperature bake crackers in the oven on a cookie sheet using the lowest setting and a thermometer. The quick method is to grind the sunflower seeds without soaking.

Herbal Flax Crackers

1 cup Flax Seeds, soaked for 8 hours in 2 cups of water
2 cups combined, Sunflower Seeds, Pumpkin Seeds, Almonds, soaked, drained, rinsed
2 cups Red Pepper, Celery, Tomato, Zucchini or Sun-dried-Tomatoes (combination)
3-4 T. dried herbs of your choice: Basil, Oregano, Curry, Garlic, Onion, Thyme, Cilantro or Dill or you may use 8 T. fresh herbs
1 T. Nutritional Yeast, optional if you want a cheese-like flavor
1 T. Sea Salt

> Flaxseeds are valuable for elimination, contain prussic acid which aids digestion, provides omega-3 fatty acids which function as an anti-inflammatory agents and provide lignans that inhibit tumor growth.

Puree: selected vegetables in the food processor with herbs and sea salt. Blend nuts and seeds, one cup at a time into the vegetable puree to mix evenly. Blend in the flax seeds that have become gelatinous. Spread the cracker mixture on a teflex dehydrator sheet evenly about ¼-inch in thickness. Dry the crackers for 8 hours and then flip them over on to a screen dehydrator sheet for another 8-10 hours until they are dry. If you don't have a dehydrator you may bake them on the lowest temperature in your oven with the door open. Use a cookie sheet, spread them on parchment paper and dry until crisp texture is achieved. Store in sealed container. They will keep for approximately 6 months.

NOTES

MORE RECIPES

Rejuvelac Recipe & Rejuvenade Recipes

Fermented Drinks

Rejuvelac is a slightly fermented, predigested, probiotic beverage that contains a high level of enzymes and nutrients. Rejuvelac provides a natural source of lactic acid which supports the proper Ph environment for maintaining healthy micro-flora in the G.I. tract, known to establish a strong immune system. Additionally, Rejuvelac contains whole complex vitamins B, C and E and is supercharged with electrolytes and other antioxidants. Rejuvelac tones the kidneys as it builds and regulates body fluids. It directly nourishes the heart, balances the mind supports emotional stability, reducing stress and irritability, insomnia, menopausal difficulty and anxiousness.

MORE RECIPIES - FERMENTED DRINKS
Sprouting Process

Buckwheat Groats are not actually a grain rather a seed of a fruit bearing plant. They are gluten-free and provide all eight essential amino acids making it a good vegetarian source of sulfur-containing amino acids which supports phase-two detoxification pathway. Buckwheat neutralizes acid waste in the body and supplies an ample source of the flavonoid, Rutin which strengthens blood vessels, increases blood flow and performs as a protective antioxidant.

Kamut is an ancient strain of wheat that has not been hybridized like traditional wheat. Many people who can't tolerate the gluten found in common wheat are able to substitute Kamut with no food sensitivity response. Kamut is higher in protein than common wheat and provides an assortment of B vitamins, vitamin A and minerals. If you have a wheat intolerance I suggest you sprout buckwheat as an alternative to sprouting Kamut to make your rejuvelac.

Sprouting Process
One cup of Buckwheat groats or one cup of Kamut. Either choice will provide two cups of sprouts. If you are using Buckwheat, cover the groats with water and soak for a period of 4-6 hours in a gallon jar. If you are using Kamut cover with water and soak for 8-10 hours. After initial soak time, drain off the soak water and rinse. Leave the seeds or grain in the gallon jar, cover the jar with cheesecloth, held tightly in place with a strong rubber band. Turn the jar on its side and gently shake to evenly distribute the soaked seeds or grain in the jar. Lay the jar down on its side, away from the direct sun. Rinse and drain the seeds/grain 2-3 times per day, never allowing water to pool inside the jar. After 2-3 days you will see sprouts with ¼-½ inch tails. You are now ready to make Rejuvelac. Sprouts will store in the refrigerator for 4-5 days. The sprouting and culturing process is quicker in warmer weather, or if you have a warming device to use in the winter, such as a dehydrator or heating pad.

MORE RECIPIES - FERMENTED DRINKS
Rejuvelac

Rejuvelac

2 cups of sprouts
¼-½ t. Probiotic
1 Gallon purified water

See Sprouting Process on page 106

> Rejuvelac is a refreshing wonderful beverage also used as a natural sports drink. It provides electrolytes the body can use for hydration. You can use lemon and/or lime juice and sweeten it with agave, stevia or raw honey.

Place the rinsed sprouts in a gallon jar, add the probiotic and water. Use a wooden spoon to stir. Replace the top with cheesecloth and a strong rubber band. Put the jar in a warm environment for 8-10 hours, room temperature is OK too. After 8-10 hours of culturing, your first batch of Rejuvelac is ready. Pour and strain through the cheese cloth into another gallon jar. Cover with a tight lid and store in the refrigerator. For your second batch of Rejuvelac retain the sprouts and probiotic in the jar. Fill the jar with water and let it culture for another 8-10 hours. You don't need to add more sprouts or probiotic. After 8-10 hours strain off your second gallon-batch of Rejuvelac into another clean jar, cover and store in refrigerator. You may repeat this process one more time, however the third time, allow it to culture for 24 hours. You receive three gallons of Rejuvelac from one set of sprouts and probiotic. It will store in the refrigerator, covered, for up to six weeks. Always check and make sure there is no mold growing in the beverage before consuming. Once you have poured off the liquid, the fermentation process slows down, so you can leave it sitting on your counter for three or four days, if you prefer a room temperature beverage. Always look and smell the Rejuvelac, before consuming to make sure it has not spoiled.

Lemon Fruit Rejuvenade

> You may also use Rejuvelac as a base for your smoothie drinks as it protects the nutrients, found in the food, from oxidizing. Rejuvelac aids in the digestion and assimilation of nutrients.

Lemon Fruit Rejuvenade

1 Banana
1 Lemon, peel removed, leaving as much of the inside white peel intact
3 T. Coconut oil
1 Pear, Apple or Strawberry (1 cup)
2½ cups Rejuvelac
3 T. Agave (optional)
5 drops Vanilla Stevia

Place: all of the ingredients into a blender and blend until smooth. Pour and Serve.

MORE RECIPIES - FERMENTED DRINKS
Frozen Lime Mint Rejuvenade

Frozen Lime Mint Rejuvenade

1 Lime, peeled, leaving inner white peel
1 Banana, frozen or fresh
4 Mint Leaves, fresh
1 Bosc Pears
3 T. Agave
5 drops Vanilla Stevia
2½ cups of Rejuvelac

> Mint is a rich source of chlorophyll which aides the body in the elimination of toxins. It functions as an anti-microbial and contains a special phytonutrient called perillyl alcohol, shown to inhibit colon, lung and skin cancer cells.

Place all ingredients into the blender and blend until smooth. You may add ice if you want it extra cold and frozen. Strawberries are also a great addition to this recipe.

NOTES

MORE RECIPES

Berry Pie, Fudgy Carob Fondue, Almond Energy Balls, Mango Pudding

Desserts

The Dessert recipes in this section are for everyone who loves a sweet treat and will satisfy any sugar craving. These special delights will not interrupt your cleanse. They are alkalizing and will assist you in the cleansing process. Eat slowly, enjoy and avoid over indulging. Eat desserts away from a meal and earlier in the day as opposed to after the dinner meal for supporting a strong digestive system. If your goal is to shed a few pounds you want to eat smaller amounts of dessert or skip them for now.

MORE RECIPIES - DESSERTS
Berry Pie

> Strawberries supply ellagic acid, an anti-tumor compound, phytonutrients which act as antioxidants which perform as anti-inflammatory agents. They naturally cleanse the body & promote elimination.

Berry Pie
Crust:
1 cup Pecans, soaked 8 hours, drained, rinsed
½ cup Almonds, soaked 8 hours, drained, rinsed
½ cup Medjool Dates, pitted
½ t. Pumpkin Spice Mix
½ t. Nama Shoyu

Filling:
3 pints of fresh Strawberries and/or Blueberries
½ cup Orange Juice, fresh
¾ cup Medjool Dates, pitted
4 t. Psyllium Powder
½ cup Coconut, shredded
1 T. Lemon Juice, hand squeezed
1 t. Cinnamon

Crust:
Chop: nuts in food processor, being careful to not over-process. Add the rest of the crust ingredients to the nuts and blend, leaving some crunchy consistency for a nutty-crunchy-crust. Press blended nut mixture into a pie pan and refrigerate.

Filling:
Blend: one cup of berries with the orange juice, dates, coconut, lemon juice, cinnamon and psyllium powder to smooth consistency. If it is not sweet enough for you, add 1-2 tablespoons of agave, raw honey or a few more dates. Hand-stir in one cup of berries into the smooth mixture, for texture. Pour into pie crust and refrigerate for at least 2 hours or until pie sets.

Fudgy Carob or Chocolate Fondue

1 cup Almond Butter, raw
1 cup raw Medjool Dates, pitted
½ cup Purified Water, warmed
1 t. Vanilla Extract
1 T. Nama Shoyu
1 ½ cups raw Carob Powder or ½ cup raw Chocolate Powder, or combination of the two powders.

> Raw Chocolate provides anandaminde, a "bliss" compound, & PEA, which keeps serotonin, dopamine and anandamide circulating longer in the brain. This combo stimulates "happy feelings", combats depression, & increases energy levels.

Blend: all ingredients in the food processor to a smooth paste, adding additional water, one tablespoon at a time to reach desired consistency. Dip fresh fruits such as apples, strawberries, pears, bananas or grapes.

Serving Note: This is a wonderful dessert to take to a party and kids love it. Recipe can be stored in the refrigerator for up to ten days.

MORE RECIPIES - DESSERTS
Almond Energy Balls

> Hemp Nut Seeds are a powerhouse of nutrients. Omega-3 EFAs, GLA, for brain function & reducing systemic inflammation. ¼ cup yields 11g. of raw protein, for proper hormone, muscle & enzyme production & function.

Almond Energy Balls
2 cups Medjool Dates, pitted
¼ cup Almond Butter, raw
¼ t. Sea Salt
¼ cup Hemp Nut Seeds
¼ cup Shredded Coconut

Place: the pitted dates in the food processor with salt and almond butter. Process until smooth, which can take several minutes. Roll them into balls. Put hemp nut seeds and/or shredded coconut on a plate. Roll the energy balls in the seeds and/or shredded coconut. Store in airtight container in the refrigerator.

Food Preparation: A variation is to add ¼ cup raw chocolate or carob powder to the food processor before you roll them. Oftentimes I make both varieties by doubling the recipe and beginning without the cocoa powder. After I roll the first half of the recipe, I add the raw cocoa or carob powder to the remaining amount and then finish rolling them. It's nice to have two flavor options. They can be rolled in hempseeds or shredded coconut.

MORE RECIPIES - DESSERTS

Mango Pudding

1 T. Golden Flax Seeds
1 T. Chia Seeds
1 Mango, ripe
1 T. Agave
¼ t. Vanilla
Nutmeg, pinch
Lemon or Lime Zest

> Chia Seeds are 20% protein, 60% omega-3 EFAs, provides fat & water-soluble antioxidants which protect healthy tissues. Chia Seeds are rich in hylauronic acid for maximum hydration and maintaining "Youthfulness".

Powder: the flax and chia seeds in a spice or coffee grinder. Peel the mango and remove the seed. Put all of the ingredients into a food processor and process until smooth consistency. Pour into your favorite dessert cups or martini glasses and chill for 30 minutes or longer. Top with zest and garnish with a fresh mint leaf.

Serving Note: You can serve with strawberries, raspberries, blueberries or any seasonal fruit.

NOTES

INGREDIENTS

GLOSSARY

GLOSSARY - INGREDIENTS

Acai is one of the top super foods in the world. Acai is a palm fruit which is grown in the Brazilian Amazon Rainforest. Acai provides rich anti-oxidant anthocyanins, which are known to slow down the aging process, support cardio vascular and digestive health. Acai contains 10-30 times the anthocyanins as red wine. Acai is a source of dietary fiber and nine essential fatty-acids. Other nutrients found in Acai include vitamins A, C and the minerals calcium and iron. Acai has additionally been used to strengthen the immune system, minimize inflammation, boost energy levels, enhance vision and promote healthy sleep habits. Serving Size: 100 grams, Calories: 130g, Protein: 2g, Carbs: 20g, Fat: 1g, Fiber: 3.5

Agave is a delicious liquid syrup sweetener that does not escalate blood sugar levels. The sugar in agave is inulin from fructose. Serving Size: 2T. Calories: 60, Protein: 0g, Carbs: 16g, Fat: 0g, Fiber: 1g

Almonds are the most alkalizing of all varieties of nuts. Their dense nutritional aspect is perfect for building and strengthening the body. Almonds provide a natural source of laetrile and amygdalin, an anticancer compound. They are valuable for building strong bones, teeth, nerves and a healthy reproductive system. Serving Size: ¼ cup, Calories: 206, Protein: 8g, Carbs: 7g, Fat: 18g, Fiber: 4g

Apples provide a high source of pectin, a soluble fiber as well as an insoluble fiber, which regulates cholesterol levels. This reduces stroke, hardening of the arteries and heart attack. Eating 2 apples a day has shown to reduce cholesterol levels by 16%. Additionally they are rich in antioxidants including vitamin C, the carotenoids beta-carotene and beta cryptoxanthin. Apples also provide flavonoids, catechin, epicatechin and quercetin along with phytosterols. These nutrients support lung health. Apples are one of the fruits that are sprayed heavily with herbicides and pesticides so purchase them organically grown as often as possible. Serving Size: 1, Calories: 65, Protein: 3g, Carbs: 17g, Fat: 0g, Fiber: 3g

GLOSSARY - INGREDIENTS

Apple Cider Vinegar is beneficial for internal cleansing as it is alkalizing to the system and does not produce acidic waste in the body. It works as a natural digestive aid, aides the body with the absorption of minerals and provides potassium, which regulates blood pressure. Serving Size: 2T., Calories: 0, Protein: 0g, Carbs: 0g, Fat: 0g, Fiber: 0g

Arame Seaweed is a variety of kelp, closely related to Wakame and Kombu. It has a mild sweet taste and is healing to the spleen, pancreas and stomach. Arame is concentrated in iron, calcium and iodine and is known to benefit the female endocrine system and will regulate blood pressure. Serving Size: 100 g, Calories: 49, Protein: 2g, Carbs: 30g, Fat: 0g, Fiber: 30g

Asparagus provides more glutathione, the liver's main antioxidant, than any other food. It not only protects the liver from tissue damage it prevents cancer. The aspartic acid, an amino acid, found in asparagus neutralizes and prevents the toxic build up of ammonia, known to cause physical weakness and tiredness. Asparagus contains asparagine which dissolves oxalic and uric acid crystals, preventing build up in the bladder, kidneys and muscles. Asparagus has a high water and roughage content which is an excellent bowel cleanser. It provides chlorophyll that effectively cleans and oxygenates the blood, rutin used for building strong veins and vitamins A, C, B1, B2, B3 and the trace mineral selinium. The combination of these nutrients protects the body from cancer. Serving Size: 100g, Calories: 43g, Protein: 3g, Carbs: 8g, Fat: 5g, Fiber: 4g

Avocado is one of nature's perfect foods. It is neither too acidic nor too alkaline. It contains a unique fruit oil, that contributes to beautiful skin and hair. Avocado is easily digested unless the liver has difficulty digesting fat and then it should be eaten in smaller amounts. It contains copper and iron that builds the blood and is a good source of protein and beneficial fat. Additional nutrients include, carotenoids, flavonoids, phytosterols and the vitamins B6, folate, C and K. Serving Size: 100g, Calories: 177, Protein: 3g, Carbs: 10g, Fat: 22g, Fiber: 7g

GLOSSARY - INGREDIENTS

Bananas are a cooling sweet fruit that lubricates the body by building essential fluids. Bananas are easily digested, soothe the stomach in case of inflammation or ulcers and are a good source of energy. Bananas contain a high amount of fiber, which relieves constipation and feeds healthy intestinal bacteria. They provide nutrients, which build and support the muscular system. Banana vitamins include C, A, B1, B2, B3, which aid in energy production and B6 which supports the nervous system as it is a component for producing serotonin, melatonin, epinephrine, norepinephrine and GABA. B6 is required for the absorption of B12. Minerals include iron, potassium, phosphorus, magnesium, sodium and calcium. Serving Size: 1, Calories: 108, Protein: 1g, Carbs: 27g, Fat: 0g, Fiber: 2g

Basil is power packed with flavonoids, which function as antioxidants. It contains volatile phytonutrients that work as an anti-inflammatory and antibacterial. Basil is plentiful in carotenoids, chlorophyll, vitamins K and C and the minerals potassium, calcium, manganese, magnesium and iron. Serving Size: 2t., Calories: 8, Protein: .44g, Carbs: 2, Fat: 1g, Fiber: 1g

Bee Pollen is the small seed found on the stamen of flower blossoms. The pollen attaches to the legs of honeybees when they are traveling from flower to flower looking for nectar. The bees secrete nectar and special enzymes into the flower pollen which creates the bee pollen. Bee pollen contains 16 vitamins, 27 minerals, 22 amino acids (all essential so it is a form of complete protein), EFAs, enzymes, co-enzymes, and hormones. It is especially rich in B vitamins including B6, B5, foliate and B12, antioxidants, including lycopene, selenium, beta carotene, vitamin C, vitamin E, and several flavanoids. Minerals include zinc, copper, iodine and manganese. It is composed of 55% carbohydrates, 35% protein, 3% vitamins and minerals, 2% fatty acids, and 5% other substances. Overall, it's one of the most nutritionally complete natural substances found on earth. Most people notice an increase in energy when they begin consuming bee pollen. Used consistently bee pollen improves your energy, stamina, endurance and over all well-being. Bee pollen can be used for weight control as it assists the thyroid in correcting a metabolic imbalance, involved in abnormal weight gain. Bee Pollen is a valuable source of iodine, which the thyroid requires for normal function. It

GLOSSARY - INGREDIENTS

contains a high percentage of natural lecithin that helps dissolve and flush fat from the body while balancing cholesterol levels. Bee Pollen supplies phenylalanine, the amino acid that naturally suppresses the appetite. The amino acids within Bee Pollen are precursors to Human Growth Hormone (HGH). Bee Pollen provides a gonadotropic hormone which is similar to the human pituitary hormone called gonadotropin. Gonadotropin functions as a sex gland hormone. Bee pollen is restorative and supportive to the female reproductive system and offers relief from PMS symptoms. Bee Pollen can be useful to people suffering from seasonal allergies as the bee pollen can strengthen and balance the immune system, so it does not over react. Serving Size: 1 t., Calories: 10, Protein: 1g, Carbs: 2g, Fat: 0g, Fiber: 4g

Black Pepper stimulates the taste buds and signals the stomach to secrete hydrochloric acid, increasing digestive power. Hydrochloric acid is essential for protein digestion and creating the acid Ph for digesting other types of foods. When HCL is insufficient, food can go undigested in the stomach causing indigestion. If food is not properly digested in the stomach it may pass through the intestines in pieces. Pathogenic bacteria can metabolize undigested food producing gas, diarrhea or constipation. Black pepper performs as an antioxidant and has demonstrated antibacterial effects. Black pepper is stimulating to the metabolism and helps breakdown and burn fat cells. Black pepper contains manganese, iron, vitamin K and fiber. Serving Size: 2t., Protein: 0g, Carbs: 1g, Fat: 0g, Fiber: 0g.

Blueberry taste is sweet, sour and loaded with anti-oxidants. Blueberries are natural in antiseptic qualities and natural cleansing agents. They are recommended for anemia, obesity, menstrual disorders, poor skin quality and balancing elimination. Blueberries are exceptional for the prevention of urinary tract infections. Blueberry vitamins include A, C, B1, B2, B3 and the minerals calcium, magnesium, phosphorus, sodium, potassium and iron. Serving Size: ½ cup raw, Calories: 83, Protein: 0g, Carbs: 21g, Fat: 0g, Fiber: 3.5g

Burdock Root is concentrated in vitamins and minerals, especially iron so it is a wonderful food for cleansing and building the blood. Burdock roots overall action on the body is

GLOSSARY - INGREDIENTS

purification as it neutralizes and removes noxious substances from the body. It is used to cleanse the inner membranes of glandular tissue as well as the elimination organs. Burdock root is used to cleanse the skin, will aide in the healing process of boils and acne, stimulate the metabolism and functions as a powerful antitumor agent. Serving Size: 10g, dried, Calories: 20, Protein: 2g, Carbs: 1g, Fat: 0g, Fiber: 1g

Cardamom is a warming digestive spice that is a good source of vitamin C, calcium, magnesium, potassium, zinc, iron. Serving Size: 1t., Calories: 6, Protein: 0g, Carbs: 0g, Fat: 0g, Fiber: 2g

Carrots are known to produce one of the highest sources of provitamin A, which can be converted into the active vitamin A form, used to increase vision and boost the immune system. They contain quercitin, one of the body's favorite antioxidants, vitamin C, B1, B3, B6, fiber and numerous essential minerals. Serving Size: 1 cup, Calories: 52, Protein: 1g, Carbs: 12g, Fat: 2g, Fiber: 7g

Cashews are related to mango and pistachio. They provide essential fatty acids, vitamins K and foliate the minerals calcium, magnesium, potassium, manganese, iron, phosphorus, selenium and copper. Serving Size: 1 oz., Calories: 155, Protein: 5g, Carbs: 9g, Fat: 12g, Fiber: 1g

Celery contains a compound known as phthalides, known to relax the muscles of major arteries, which regulates blood pressure, by allowing the vessels to dilate. The high levels of potassium also support the heart and healthy blood pressure. It is a rich source of vitamin C, flavonoids and coumarins known to boost the immune system and protect the body from dangerous cancerous cells. Serving Size: 1 cup, Calories: 19, Protein: 1g, Carbs: 4g, Fat: 0g, Fiber: 4g

GLOSSARY - INGREDIENTS

Chia Seeds contain 60% omega 3 (ALA) anti-inflammatory essential fatty acids; 20% complete protein; Anti-oxidants including vitamin C, E, cinnamic acid, quercitin, myricetin, chlorogenic acid, caffeic acid, flavanols; Minerals-calcium, magnesium, iron, zinc, potassium. They provide a source of slow burning carbohydrates that increases stamina and endurance; hylauronic acid (absorbs 9x its volume in liquid) that promotes internal hydration, maintains and balances essential electrolytes. They are high in soluble fiber which promotes motility and eliminates waste. Chia seeds facilitate growth and tissue repair. Serving Size: 1 oz., Calories: 137, Protein: 4g, Carbs: 12g, Fat: 1g, Fiber: 11g

Chocolate Powder (raw Cacao) contains many chemicals that enhance physical and mental well-being, including an incredibly rich supply of magnesium. Magnesium relaxes nerves and muscles, strengthens bones and assists smooth blood flow. Studies show that eighty percent of Americans are magnesium deficient. Additionally, magnesium supports healthy stabilized blood pressure and overall cardiovascular function. Raw chocolate powder contains other chemicals that enhance physical and mental well-being. These include alkaloids, proteins with the amino acids leucine and lysine, and the enzyme lipase. Raw Cacao provides the neurotransmitter dopamine, anandamide known as the bliss chemical and PEA which keeps dopamine and seratonin circulating longer in the brain. It contains theobromine, which is simular to caffeine. Theobromine stimulates the Central Nervous System, dilates blood vessels and relaxes smooth muscle tissues. Theobromine is only 1/4 of the simulant of caffeine. Raw Cacao contains monoamine oxidase, an enzyme inhibitor that maintains seratonin, dopamine and anandamide levels. Serving size 1T., Calories: 15g, Protein: 2g, Carbs: 3g, Fat: 1.5g, Fiber: 2g

Cilantro is an aromatic herb that contains chlorophyll and fiber along with the vitamins B1, B2, B3, B5, B6, Foliate, A, C, E, K and the minerals calcium, magnesium, potassium, copper, iron, manganese. Cilantro is detoxifying to the system as it removes heavy metals from the body. Serving Size: 2T., Calories: 46, Protein: 2g, Carbs: 3g, Fat: 0g, Fiber: .06g

GLOSSARY - INGREDIENTS

Cinnamon is a warm digestive aid that assists in stabilizing blood sugar levels while increasing sensitivity to insulin. Cinnamaldehyde, the essential oil and active component functions as an anti-microbial killing fungus and yeast growth. It works as an anti-inflammatory as it inhibits the inflammatory fatty acid called arachidonic acid. Cinnamaldehyde is also useful in the blood stream as it prevents excessive platelet clumping and balances cholesterol levels. Cinnamon provides fiber, vitamin C, choline, iron, manganese and thiamine. Manganese is essential for thyroid function and strong bones. The antioxidants in cinnamon work as a food preservative. Serving size: 2t., Calories: 12, Protein: 0g, Carbs: 0g, Fat: 0g, Fiber: 3g

Cloves help relax the smooth muscles of the digestive tract, are warming to the system and aid in digestion as they prevent gas. They are an anti-fungal and destroy parasites. Cloves are a great source of manganese and a good source of EFAs, Vitamin C, K and fiber. Serving Size: 2t., Calories 14, Protein: 0g, Carbs: 0g, Fat: 0g, Fiber: 3g

Coconut Cream or **Coconut Butter** is whole coconut meat in concentrated form. It contains no additives or water. The dried coconut meat is ground into a very fine powder, giving it a creamy consistency due to its high fat content. It is 70% fat and it is a rich source of pure coconut oil. Use this as a food only. It is not suitable as cooking oil. You can mix 1-2 teaspoons of Coconut Cream with water or juice to make a creamy coconut milk drink. It can be used to enhance soups, be blended into smoothies, or made into ice cream. Serving size: 1 t., Calories: 31, Protein: 3g, Carbs: 1.1g, Fat: 3g, Fiber: 1g

Coconut oil is a medium chain triglyceride/good fat source containing 50-55% Lauric acid that supports metabolism. It is shelf stable for up to five years (no need to refrigerate). Lauric acid is predominant in Mother's milk and is converted into monolaurin in the body where it strengthens the immune system. Monolaurin destroys lipid coated viruses such as HIV, influenza and herpes as well as heliobacteria (ulcers) and giardia lamblia. Functions as an antifungal and reduces candida. Medium Chain Fatty Acids (MCFA) speed up metabolism as they do not require bile salts to digest, they are not stored in the liver and are bio-available for instant energy release, placing less strain on the liver, pancreas and digestive system. Coconut oil regulates blood sugar and is the ideal fat for people dealing with diabetes. Additionally, coconut oil detoxifies the liver, builds healthy lipoproteins (LDL and HDL), provides a healthy raw material for producing hormones, fats (for cellular repair and reproduction) and bile for fat digestion and assimilation of vitamin A, D, E and K (prevents osteoporosis). Coconut oil protects the skin from skin cancer and wrinkling as coconut oil is stable in heat and oxygen. The small molecular structure is easily absorbed through the skin promoting softness, while reducing skin inflammation. MCFA helps prevent heart disease (does not promote sticky blood platelets), stroke and hardening of the arteries. Coconut oil is a great source of iodine which promotes functionality of thyroid, reducing hypothyroidism. Make sure to purchase non-hydrogenated organic extra virgin coconut oil. Serving Size: 1 T., Calories: 120, Protein: 0g, Carbs: 0, Fat: 14g, Fiber: 0

Coconut water is identical to human blood plasma which makes up 55% of human blood. Coconut water hydrates the body and is one of the highest sources of essential natural electrolytes. Electrolytes provide nervous system and muscular energy. Serving Size: 11 oz., Calories: 60, Protein: 1g, Carbs: 15g, Fat: 0, Fiber: 0g

Cucumber is an alkalizing cooling food that neutralizes and excretes acids from the blood and tissues, through the bladder and kidneys, reducing stones. Cucumbers contain a special enzyme known as erepsin. Erepsin aides in protein digestion and destroys tapeworms in the intestines. Cucumbers are a wonderful source of silicon, essential for calcium absorption, vitamin A and C, chlorophyll, potassium and fiber. Serving Size: 1 cup, Calories: 13, Protein: 1g, Carbs: 3g, Fat: 1g, Fiber: 1g

Cumin strengthens digestion and stimulates the production of digestive juices. Cumin increases blood circulation, prevents and relieves flatulence and cramping in the intestines. Serving Size: 10g, Calories: 3, Protein: 0g, Carbs: 0g, Fat: 0g, Fiber: 0g

GLOSSARY - INGREDIENTS

Dill is a member of the parsley family. Dill contains a volatile oil known as carvone that has been used medicinally for its ability to calm the stomach, relieve spasms and remove excess fluids from the body. Carvone is a remedy for reducing blood glucose levels, as it balances the hormone insulin. Dill is also used as a digestive aide and prevents flatulence.
Serving Size: 10g, Calories: 1, Protein: 0g, Carbs: 0g, Fat: 0g, Fiber: 0g

Eggs (raw) are a great way to get a source of protein that is easy to assimilate as well as being affordable. All protein is measured against the egg, as the egg white albumin is considered to be the perfect protein, which matches the protein in our blood. The yolk provides DHA and EPA, two essential fatty acids required for brain function. Additionally egg yolk contains choline, a nutrient similar to a B vitamin which is used to make the neurotransmitter acetylcholine. This supports mental function which includes memory and organizational skills. Choline is used by every cell to produce healthy cellular membranes and to balance homocysteine levels, which can potentially damage arteries and lead to Cardio Vascular Disease (CVD). Other nutrients in eggs include selenium, used as an anti-oxidant that boosts the immune system, Folic Acid (B9), B12 (anemia prevention) and B2 which is essential for energy production. The yolk provides vitamin A, used for skin rejuvenation and vision as well as the powerful antioxidants lutein and zeaxanthin found concentrated in the eye (prevents macular degeneration). The yolk also contains vitamin E another powerful anti-aging antioxidant. Make sure to purchase organic eggs from a reliable source. Dangers of salmonella poisoning are very rare, when purchased from a clean farm that practices humane treatment of animals. Never eat an egg with a crack in the shell. The yolk needs to be in one form so if it breaks easily, discard the egg. The white should have a gel-like consistency so discard the egg if the white is watery. If the egg smells foul don't consume it. You can roll the egg across the counter and if it rolls wobbly it is safe to eat. Some people avoid eggs because they contain cholesterol (212 mg.). Every 24 hours the liver synthesizes approximately 3000mg. of cholesterol if you don't assimilate enough from the food you eat. Cholesterol is used by the body to make all of the male and female steroidal hormones, repair cells and other damaged tissue. When cholesterol levels are too low depression can

GLOSSARY - INGREDIENTS

result. When you over cook eggs, the excessive heat temperature will break and bind the amino acids together, making it more difficult for the body to utilize. If you are cooking eggs, I recommend a soft poach. Don't eat raw eggs everyday as the avidin (glycoprotein) in the white portion of the egg is bound to biotin and can also block assimilation of biotin. Biotin belongs to the B-vitamin family and is essential for the metabolism of fats, sugars and amino acids. Biotin is a critical component of energy production for the nervous and muscular systems. Healthy production of fat cells is imperative because skin cells reproduce rapidly and they are exposed to the environment as protection. Almonds, Swiss chard, yogurt, goat milk, carrots, tomatoes, raspberries, onions, avocado, bananas, walnuts, cashews and salmon are good sources of biotin. Serving Size: 1, Calories: 70, Protein: 7g, Carbs: 0g, Fat: 4.5g, Fiber: 0g

Flax Seeds are a rich source of essential fatty acids and fiber. They provide a thick mucilaginous fluid that heals the lining of the GI tract, coats the stomach and increases elimination. Flax seeds contain eight essential amino acids, lignans known to protect women from breast cancer and prussic acid which stimulates digestion and enhances respiration. Serving Size: 10g, Calories: 5, Protein: 2g, Carbs: 1g, Fat: 1g, Fiber: 2g

Garlic is a powerful antibiotic and antifungal. Garlic contains sulfur compounds that are effective for combating various illnesses. Garlic is excellent for the entire digestive system, detoxifies heavy metals from the body, cleans the blood, kills parasites and fungus, purifies the blood and blood vessels, regulates liver function and supports the immune system. It is a source of iodine, calcium, potassium, iron, phosphorus and magnesium. Serving Size: 1 clove, Calories: 0, Protein: 0g, Carbs: 0g, Fat: 0g, Fiber: 0g

Jalapeño Pepper is a good source of vitamins including B1, B2, B3, B6, folic acid, C, A and K. It also provides the minerals magnesium, phosphorus, potassium, copper, manganese and iron. Jalapeños are powerful blood cleansers and are known to remove parasites, heavy metals and other toxins from the body. They stimulate digestion and aide in elimination due to their fiber content. Serving Size: 1, Calories: 5, Protein: .5g, Carbs: 1g, Fat: 0g, Fiber: 0g

GLOSSARY - INGREDIENTS

Lemon and **Lime** are one of the most alkalizing foods. They contain flavonoids known as hesperitin and naringenin, which promote heart and vascular health. They provide a great source of water-soluble vitamin C, which functions as an antioxidant and supports the immune system. They are a source of carotenoids and limonene a unique oil that balances the livers biotransformation process. Serving Size: 100g, Calories: 25, Protein: 0g, Carbs: 2g, Fat: 0g, Fiber: 0g

Lettuce is made of ninety to ninety-five percent water, and is a source of almost every vitamin and mineral essential to the human body. It is a rich source of silicon, which is essential for the absorption of calcium, so it is critical for bones, teeth, joints, arteries and connective tissues. Lettuce is rich in magnesium and provides a unique compound called lactucarium, which relaxes the nervous system. It is a useful food in the evening as it encourages healthy sleeping patterns and is good for fertility due to a high Vitamin E content. Serving Size: 100g, Calories: 13, Protein: 1g, Carbs: 1g, Fat: 0g, Fiber: 0g

Ginger prevents nausea, vomiting and motion sickness. Ginger is valuable as a cold remedy because it is a carminative which induces healthy sweating at the onset of a cold or flu. Ginger functions as a digestive aid as it is warming and reduces intestinal gas. The phenolic action of Gingerol suppresses pro-inflammatory compounds. This would include inflammatory compounds cytokines and chemokines (produced by synoviocytes, which are cells that make up the synovial lining of joints). Gingerol suppresses inflammatory responses produced by chrondrocytes (joint cartilage cells) and leukocytes (immune system cells). Gingerol functions as an important antioxidant that prevents damage to lipids, cell membranes and cholesterol. New studies have shown Gingerol to prevent ovarian cancer and colorectal tumors. Serving Size: 100 g, Calories: 69, Protein: 2g, Carbs: 0g, Fat: 0g, Fiber: 1g

Goji Berries contain (according to the Beijing Nutrition Research Institute) analysis, more beta carotene than carrots, and 500 times more vitamin C by weight than oranges. The fruit provides 18 amino acids, 21 trace minerals, and substantial amounts of vitamin B1, B2, B6 and vitamin E. Goji Berries have essential fatty acids and have shown to be an incredibly rich source

GLOSSARY - INGREDIENTS

of carotenoids. Additionally, they support the body with selenium and germanium, which are well-known anti-cancer agents, beta sitosterol, an anti-inflammatory agent found to lower cholesterol, and has been used to treat impotence and prostate enlargement, zeaxanthin and lutein, known to protect vision, betaine which produces choline in the liver that assists in phase one and two detoxification processes. Choline is also known to protect DNA (genetic code), enhance memory, encourage muscle growth and protects against fatty liver disease. Cyperone is another element found in Goji berries which is used in treatment of cervical cancer and shown to regulate blood pressure, heart and menstruation problems. Goji berries also provide Solavetivone an anti-bacterial and anti-fungal agent and Physalin, a compound known to boost the immune system and effective in treating leukemia, cancer and hepatitis B. Serving Size: 1 oz., Calories: 90, Protein: 4g, Carbs: 24g, Fat: 0g, Fiber: 4g

Green tea powder (Matcha) contains antioxidants properties, including polyphenols and theanine. Green tea also provides a wide variety of vitamins and minerals. Polyphenols are a class of phytochemicals found in high concentrations in green tea, and have been associated with preventing heart disease and cancer. The slight astringent, bitter taste of green tea is attributed to polyphenols. Green tea contains tannins, a group of simple and complex phenols, polyphenol, and flavonoid compounds. Green tea also contains catechins which are a category of polyphenols. In green tea, catechins are present in significant quantities, more specifically; epicatechin (EC), epigallocatechin (EGC), epicatechin gallate (ECG) and epi-gallocatechin gallate (EGCG). EGCG makes up about 10-50% of the total catechin content and appears to be the most powerful of the catechins, with antioxidant activity about 25-100 times more potent than vitamins C and E. A cup of green tea may provide 10-40mg of polyphenols and has antioxidant activity greater than a serving of broccoli, spinach, carrots or strawberries. Flavonoids are plant pigments, brightly colored chemical constituents found in most fresh fruits and vegetables. Flavonoids prevent infection and promote vascular health. A flavonoid deficiency can result in a tendency to bruise easily. Green tea also contains theanine which is an amino acid that produces tranquilizing effects in the brain. Two cups of green tea has approximately twice the antioxidants of red wine, 7 times that of orange juice, & 20 times that of apple juice. Serving Size: 1oz., Calories: 90, Protein: 4g, Carbs: 24g, Fat: 0g, Fiber: 4g

GLOSSARY - INGREDIENTS

Matcha Green Tea Powder benefits include:

- Antioxidants: which are natural compounds that help, protect the body from harmful free radicals, which are believed to be the cause of destruction & death in nearly all living things. Free radicals can attack, damage, & ultimately destroy cellular tissues and DNA.
- Increases your metabolism - helps to loose weight
- Protects against cancer
- Bolsters your immune defenses
- Less caffeine than coffee
- May reduce your risk of heart attack & stroke
- Helps protect your bones & prevent tooth decay
- Helps to keep you hydrated

Serving Size: ½t., Protein: 0g, Carbs: 0g, Fat: 0g, Fiber: 0g

Hemp protein powder is a great way to go when you want to increase the protein in your shake. Hemp protein powder contains 19 amino acids, 9 of which are essential. Hemp protein powder is the highest vegetarian source of absorbable protein with the presence of edestin-65% and 35-% albumin, identical to human blood. Hemp contains two sulfur containing amino acids (methionine and cysteine) which are essential in the Phase Two Detoxification process used by the liver to convert dangerous fat soluble toxins into toxic waste that can be eliminated by the body. High level branched-chain amino acids contained in Hemp provide the body with building blocks for growing and repairing a lean healthy body. Hemp is a source of well-balanced essential fatty acids, enzymes and minerals including a high source of magnesium, calcium, iron, sulfur, phosphorus, zinc, sodium and potassium. Hemp provides cleansing chlorophyll and B vitamins. Other nutrients include choline, inositol, lecithin, vitamin E and phytosterols. Hemp is low in carbohydrates and high in soft soluble fiber. Add two heaping scoops to any favorite smoothie recipe. Serving Size: 2T. (30 g), Calories: 67, Protein: 8g, Carbs: 2g, Fat: 3g, Fiber: 2g

INSIDE BACK COVER

Kale is an excellent source of vitamin C. One cup of kale supplies approximately 90% of the RDA for vitamin C. Vitamin C is the primary water-soluble antioxidant in the body. Vitamin C disarms free radicals which prevents damage both inside and outside cells. Free radical damage inside the cell, to DNA (genetic code), may potentially result in cancer. Cellular turnover happens quickly in the digestive system, so this is one area where antioxidant protection from free radicals is required, to prevent colon cancer. Free radical damage to cellular structures can result in painful inflammation. Vitamin C has shown to prevent free radical damage that triggers an inflammatory response in conditions such as asthma, osteoarthritis, and rheumatoid arthritis. Free radicals also oxidize cholesterol. Oxidized cholesterol sticks to artery walls, creating a build up in plaque which may block blood flow, causing a heart attack or stroke. Vitamin C can squelch free radicals, and help prevent the oxidation of cholesterol. Vitamin C is essential for the proper function of a healthy immune system as white blood cells must have it for proper function. Vitamin C and sugar compete for absorption so sugar inhibits the proper absorption of Vitamin C and suppresses the immune system. Vitamin C prevents colds and reoccurring infections. Kale provides a wonderful source of vitamin A, which is essential to lung health. People who smoke are often deficient in vitamin A, which leads to lung disease. Kale provides the trace element manganese which helps produce energy from protein and carbohydrates. It is involved in the synthesis of fatty acids that are important for a healthy nervous system and in the production of cholesterol that is used by the body to produce sex hormones. Manganese is also a critical component for the antioxidant enzyme called superoxide dismutase (SOD). SOD is found inside the body's mitochondria which is the oxygen-based energy factory inside the cell. SOD neutralizes free radical damage that is produced during energy production. Kale (leafy greens) contain high amounts of vitamin E complex, which supports brain function, cell signaling (communication between cells), prevents oxidative stress in healthy tissue and protects the skin from UV light damage. To receive maximum health benefits from leafy greens consume at least 3 serving (1 cup equals 1 serving) per day. They can easily be blended into smoothies. When you consume fat soluble vitamins with oil (coconut oil, for example) absorption is increased. Kale contains an enzyme called myrosinase which converts

GLOSSARY - INGREDIENTS

dormant plant nutrients into their active state. Breaking down the cell wall in a blender or cutting it into thin slices activates myrosinase. Vitamin C increases the enzyme activity, which is provided in fruit. Cooking kale destroys myrosinase. Kale is a wonderful source of fiber for motility and the elimination of toxins and waste. Additional vitamins found in kale include vitamin K and folic acid. Minerals provided in kale include calcium, magnesium, phosphorus, potassium, sodium and iron. Serving Size: 1 cup, Calories: 37, Protein: 3g, Carbs: 7g, Fat: 0g, Fiber: 3g

Mango provides soft soluble fiber which aides in elimination, provides vitamins C, carotenoids which are valuable for eye sight, B6 and foliate essential for maintaining homocysteine levels. Mango is a good source of Choline for brain activity, including memory. Minerals include calcium, magnesium, phosphorus and potassium. Mangos provide a healthy source of omega 3 essential fatty-acids. Serving Size: 1, Calories: 63, Protein: 1g, Carbs: 28g, Fat: 0g, Fiber: 1g

Medjool Dates are sweet, delicious and easy to digest. Medjool dates provide a good source of energy and can be used to make wonderful treats instead of eating processed sugar. Medjool dates are a source of vitamin A along with the minerals calcium, magnesium, phosphorus, potassium and iron. Serving Size: 100g, Calories: 142, Protein: 2g, Carbs: 37, Fat: 0, Fiber: 4g

Mint contains volatile oils and functions as a stimulant, tonic, aromatic and stomachic. It is a powerful digestive aide which regulates stomach, liver, gallbladder and intestine activity. Mint is known to regulate sexual function, prevents intestinal gas, nausea and vomiting. It is effective for killing parasites and has numerous cleansing properties. Mint is rich in minerals including calcium, iron, magnesium, phosphorus, potassium and vitamins B1, B2, B3, C and A. Serving Size: 10g, Calories: 0, Protein: 0g, Carbs: 0g, Fat: 0g, Fiber: 0g

Miso is typically an unpasteurized fermented paste made from a combination of water, sea salt, soybeans and grains or rice. Miso can be purchased gluten free and is high in

GLOSSARY - INGREDIENTS

enzymes, B vitamins and contains friendly bacteria. It is important to use warm water so you don't destroy the friendly bacteria. Serving Size: 1t., Calories: 10, Protein: 1g, Carbs: 1g, Fat: 0g, Fiber: 0g

Mushrooms are lacking in sugar as the carbohydrates are from a source of cellulose. There are many varieties of mushrooms, some of which need to be cooked to destroy carcinogens (found in common mushrooms). Shiitake and Crimini mushrooms are a wonderful B vitamin source, stimulate the immune system, prevent tumors and contain germanium known as an anti-aging agent which oxygenates the body. Mushrooms are useful for removing acidic waste stored in the body from eating animal protein. Serving Size: 100g, Calories: 55, Protein: 2g, Carbs: 2g, Fat: 0g Fiber: 2g

Mustard Seed stimulates digestion and promotes a cleansing action as it contains sulfur which removes stagnant toxins and impurities from the blood and tissues. Serving Size: 1t, Calories: 15, Protein: 0g, Carbs: 0g, Fat: 0g, Fiber: 0g

Olives are a concentrated form of fat and have a tendency to slow down body function, especially in the liver. They are appropriate for people who are burning food rapidly and have nervous energy or a type "A" personality. Olives contain squalene, a functional compound found in the human body and a precursor to all steroidal hormonal production, in the adrenal glands. Squalene is highly concentrated in the skin, where it provides protection from invading pathogens and is used to oxygenate the body. Olives are a rich source of vitamin E and A known to regenerate the skin. Serving Size: 15g (3), Calories: 20, Protein: 0g, Carbs: 1g, Fat: 2g, Fiber: 1g

Olive Oil is easily digested and soothes the entire GI tract. Olive oil strengthens vital tissues and benefits the liver and gallbladder with a cleansing action. It is healing for the nervous system, stimulates the production of bile and increases peristalsis. This action encourages elimination. Olive oil is 73% oleic acid, a fatty acid that the body uses to make nervous and cerebral tissue. It contains the identical structure of linolenic acid found in breast milk which assists with the absorption of fat soluble vitamins E and A, also found in olives.

GLOSSARY - INGREDIENTS

Linolenic fatty acid assists in the mineralization of teeth and bones. Serving Size: 1T., Calories: 120, Protein: 0g, Carbs: 0g, Fat: 2g saturated, 1g polyunsaturated, 1g, monounsaturated, 11g, Fiber: 0g

Onion balances blood pressure and cholesterol levels. It contains powerful sulfur phytonutrients, allyl propyl sulfoxides, which are responsible for the strong smell that also irritates eyes. This amazing compound balances blood sugar levels and the stronger the smell the more healing power it contains. Onions are a good source of chromium, known to balance blood sugar levels, so this is an excellent food for preventing diabetes and anti-aging. Onions provide a valuable source of flavanoids including quercitin, an anti-inflammatory and antioxidant compound. Onions are a source of vitamin A and C and the minerals potassium and phosphorus, great for the heart, bones and teeth. Serving Size: 1 cup, Calories: 60, Protein: 2g, Carbs: 14g, Fat: 2g, Fiber: 6g

Papaya (ripe) is a delicious fruit which provides a substantial amount of pro-vitamin A, carotenoids including beta-carotene, beta-cryptoxanthin, lutein and zeaxanthin, all important anti-oxidants. These nutrients are converted into fat-soluble vitamin A known to promote lung tissue and health. Papaya contains fiber, vitamin C, E, foliate, K and the minerals calcium, chloride, magnesium and potassium. Unripe green papaya provides papain, a proteolytic enzyme that digests protein when eaten with food and reduces inflammation, including allergic responses, when eaten between meals. Serving Size: 1, Calories: 118, Protein: 2g, Carbs: 30g, Fat: 0g, Fiber: 6g

Parsley is an abundant source of nutrients including chlorophyll, vitamin A, C, E, B1, B2, B3, B6 and B9 (folic acid). It provides the minerals calcium, magnesium, iron, phosphorus, potassium, sodium, zinc, copper, manganese and essential trace elements. Parsley benefits the skin, cleans the blood and blood vessels, oxygenates the body and increases bowel transit time. It eliminates bad breath, enhances hearing and relieves ear infections while promoting proper kidney function. Serving Size: 10g, Calories: 3, Protein: 0g, Carbs: 1g, Fat: 0g, Fiber: 1g

GLOSSARY - INGREDIENTS

Peaches provide a good source of fiber, vitamins C, A, K, choline and niacin. They are easily digested and low on the glycemic index so they will not over stimulate blood sugar levels. Peaches contain the minerals, calcium, magnesium, potassium and phosphorus. Peaches are alkalizing to the body, which supports beautiful skin and youth. Serving Size: 1, Calories: 43, Protein: 0g, Carbs: 19g, Fat: 0g, Fiber: 2g

Pears are an excellent source of fiber which binds to cancer causing cells in the colon and eliminates them. Pears are a source of copper which is a component of red blood cells and the antioxidant Super Oxide Dismutase (SOD). SOD is used by the immune system as part of the clean up crew, after white blood cells attack pathogens. Pears contain vitamin A, C, Folic acid, K and small amounts of B vitamins. They are a source of minerals including calcium, copper, iron, magnesium, manganese, phosphorus, potassium and selenium. Serving Size: 1, Calories: 59, Protein: 0g, Carbs: 26g, Fat: 0g, Fiber: 2g

Pineapple provides a source of bromelain, which is an enzyme that functions as a digestive aid when eaten with food and an anti-inflammatory when eaten between meals. Bromelain has shown to inhibit excessive blood clotting and reduce production of inflammatory molecules. Enzymes found in pineapple support the immune system, by breaking up proteins in undesirable bacteria and increasing messenger molecules (protection) including cytokines (tumor necrosis factor-alpha, interleukin-1-beta and interleukin-6). Ripe pineapples are rich in vitamin C, essential for immune system function, a source of beta-carotene, thiamine, the B1 vitamin which is critical for energy production and B6 which supports the nervous system as it is a component for producing serotonin, melatonin, epinephrine, norepinephrine and GABA. Serving Size: 1 cup, Calories: 75, Protein: 1g, Carbs: 19g, Fat: 0g, Fiber: 2g

Pine Nuts are a concentrated source of protein, fats, vitamins and minerals. They are an excellent source of vitamin B1, B2, B3,B6, E and the minerals manganese, copper, magnesium, zinc, iron and molybdenum . They work to suppress the appetite as they contain two important chemicals, cholecystokinin (CCK) and glucagon like peptide-1 (GLP-1), which contribute to feeling

GLOSSARY - INGREDIENTS

satiated, after consumption. Korean pine nuts in particular suppress the appetite as they contain satiety hormones. Pine nuts contain pineolenic acid, which has an effect on LDL cholesterol receptor activity as it increase the liver's uptake of LDL, reducing dangerous cholesterol levels. Pine nuts are known as a "heart healthy" food. Serving Size: 10g, Calories: 67, Protein: 4g, Carbs: 0g, Fat: 6g, Fiber: 0g

Pumpkin Seeds are known to promote men's health due to their concentrated source of zinc and magnesium. They are beneficial for removing parasites from the intestines because they contain an amino acid called 3-amino-3carboxypyrrolidine or cucurbitin. Pumpkins seeds also contain a unique oil called myosin, which aids in muscle contration. Serving Size: 10g, Calories: 55, Protein: 3g, Carbs: 0g, Fat: 2g, Fiber: 1g

Quinoa is an ancient seed that provides a high quality source of complete protein. It was the sacred principal food of the Incas. It is a high energy food that is easily digested and assimilated. It provides a good source of calcium, magnesium, iron and phosphorus. Quinoa supplies the essential amino acid lysine, which promotes tissue repair and growth. Lysine is heat sensitive and easily destroyed by cooking or manufacturing practices. Serving Size: 1 cup soaked, lightly cooked, Calories: 158, Protein: 6g, Carbs: 29g, Fat: 2g, Fiber: 3g

Red Pepper are ripened green peppers and provide a higher source of nutrients including carotenoids, vitamin C, B6 and E. They contain the minerals copper, which builds the blood and potassium excellent for heart health. Serving Size: 1 cup, raw, Calories: 25, Protein: 1g, Carbs: 6g, Fat: 0g, Fiber: 3g

Romaine Lettuce is nutritious, very low in calories and high in water content so it is a perfect diet food. Romaine is satiating as it provides an adequate source of soluble and insoluble fiber which is essential for proper elimination. Romaine lettuce contains chromium an important mineral which stabilizes blood sugar. Chromium is one of the trace elements which compose the Glucose Tolerance Factor (GTF). GTF sensitizes cells to insulin. Insulin

GLOSSARY - INGREDIENTS

is the hormone which signals cells to open and receive glucose through the cell wall. This is beneficial for the prevention of Type II Diabetes and for supporting people who have Type II Diabetes. Romaine is a great source of Folic Acid and B6 which are critical nutrients for converting homocysteine into SAMe and Glutathione. Studies show excessive levels of homocysteine in the blood damages arteries resulting in cardiovascular and heart disease, weakening the immune system and accelerating the aging process. Serving Size: 2 cups, Calories: 16, Protein: 2, Carbs: 3g, Fat: 0g, Fiber: 2g

Raspberries have a sweet and sour taste, which is beneficial to the liver and kidneys. Raspberry is a natural blood tonic as it cleanses toxins, reduces anemia, balances blood pressure, regulates menstrual flow and reduces menstrual cramps. Raspberries effect on the kidneys assists in the regulation of urine flow and cleanses the urinary tract. Raspberries destroy intestinal worms, dissolves fat build-up which stores toxins and eliminates constipation. Raspberry is plentiful in the vitamins C, A, B1, B2, B3 and the minerals calcium, magnesium, phosphorus, iron, sodium, potassium and silicon. Serving Size: 1 cup, Calories: 60, Protein: 1g, Carbs: 14g, Fat: 0g, Fiber: 8g

Sage aides in digestion and functions as an antioxidant, which prevents premature aging. It supports the female endocrine system as it balances estrogen levels and treats "hot flashes". This is due to a compound known as sclereol, which stimulates estrogen production. Sage also supports the health of the kidneys, intestines, stomach, liver, spleen, skin, scalp, hair. You can use fresh Sage to whiten teeth, by rubbing fresh leaves directly on them. This also reduces plaque, restores gums and eliminates bad breath. Sage is plentiful in volatile oils which are antimicrobial and antioxidants, phenolic acids. Avoid the use of Sage if you are pregnant or epileptic. Serving Size: 10g, Calories: 30, Protein: 1g, Carbs: 0g, Fat: 1g, Fiber: 1g

Sea Salt provides an adequate amount of alkalizing minerals and trace elements. I recommend purchasing Himalayan or Celtic Sea Salt. Serving Size: ¼ t., Calories: 0g, Protein: 0g, Carbs: 0g, Fat: 0g, Fiber: 0g

GLOSSARY - INGREDIENTS

Sesame Seeds contains a special compound called sesamol and vitamin E, both known to be natural preservatives. It is a source of monounsaturated, polyunsaturated and lecithin, all oils which build the nervous and limbic system. It increases the circulatory system, treats depression and relieves stress. The naturally occurring sesamin, a lignin phytonutrient, exists only in sesame seeds. It is known to balance cholesterol levels and prevent the re-absorption of old cholesterol which can become oxidized damage tissues and generate tumors. Serving Size: 14g, 1T. Calories: 86, Protein: 3g, Carbs: 4g, Fat: 7g, 1 saturated, Fiber: 2g

Snow Peas are rich in green chlorophyll, the vitamins B1, B2, B3, B6, B9 K and C and the minerals calcium, iron, zinc, phosphorus and potassium. They are a nourishing food for the stomach, spleen, liver and gallbladder, promote heart health and increase energy system levels. Serving Size: 1 cup, Calories: 134, Protein: 9g, Carbs: 25g, Fat: 0g, Fiber: 9g

Spinach has been identified as containing 13 different flavonoid compounds which function as antioxidants and as anti-cancer agents, shown to slow down cell division in stomach cancer cells (gastric adenocarcinomas), to reduce skin cancers (skin papillomas) and breast cancer cells. A carotenoid found in spinach and other green leafy vegetables fights human prostate cancer two different ways: The carotenoid, called neoxanthin, stimulates prostate cancer cells to self-destruct. Neoxanthin is converted in the intestines into other compounds, known as neochromes, which inhibit cancer cell replication. Research calculating the intake of a flavonoid called kaempferol with 66,940 women (the Nurses Health Study between 1984 and 2002) showed that women consuming the highest amount of kaempferol had a 40% reduction in risk of ovarian cancer, when compared to women eating the least amount of kaempferol-rich foods. In addition to spinach, foods richest in kaempferol include tea (non-herbal), onions, curly kale, leeks, broccoli, and blueberries. The vitamin K provided by one cup of spinach is approximately 200% of the RDA. Vitamin K1 activates osteocalcin, the main non-collagenous protein found in the bone. Osteocalcin plants and anchors calcium molecules inside of the bone. Vitamin K1 deficiency results in inadequate osteocalcin levels and bone mineralization is impaired. Spinach also provides a valuable source of calcium and magnesium, necessary for bone health. Spinach is an excellent source of vitamin C and vitamin A (beta-carotene), both important antioxidants which reduce free radicals in the body protecting colon cells. Vitamin C (water-soluble antioxidant) and beta-carotene (fat-soluble antioxidant) perform synergistically to prevent cholesterol from becoming oxidized. Oxidized cholesterol is dangerous to the circulatory system, as it is sticky and can adhere, and build up, in blood vessel walls. This is a well known cause of blocked arteries, heart attack and stroke. Spinach is also a source of folic acid, which is utilized in the conversion of homocysteine (an amino acid) into SAMe and Glutathione. High levels of homocysteine have been a marker for many health issues including heart attack, stroke and cancer. Foliate protects DNA in colon cells from toxic waste and damaging free radicals, resulting in colorectal cancer. Studies show that people who consume high levels of foods rich in vitamin C, beta-carotene (pro-vitamin A) and foliate have a much lower risk for colon cancer. Spinach provides a source of magnesium. Magnesium is an important mineral which balances blood pressure, provides protection against heart disease, aides in calcium absorption and relaxes nerves and muscles tissues. Nutrients in spinach, including beta-carotene and vitamin C, inhibit inflammatory conditions found in asthma, osteoarthritis and rheumatoid arthritis. The vitamin E found in spinach and other leafy greens may assist in protecting the brain from oxidative stress, memory loss and other effects of age-related declines in brain function. Serving Size: 1 cup, Calories: 41, Protein: 5g, Carbs: 7g, Fat: 0g, Fiber: 4g

Stevia is an herb from South America that stabilizes blood sugar levels. Stevia contains no calories, carbohydrates or fats so it is a great herb and sweetener for people watching their weight. Stevia has been used for hundreds of years in South America and Asia for its intense sweetening properties. Stevia is up to 300 times sweeter than sugar. Stevia can be found in various forms, as a liquid extract, liquid concentrate made of the whole stevia leaves, in powder form as well as pre-portioned packets. Serving Size: 1t., Calories: 5, Protein: 0g, Carbs: 1g, Fat: 0g, Fiber: 1g

GLOSSARY - INGREDIENTS

Strawberry produces a sweet and sour taste, which moistens mucus membrane tissues and builds natural body fluids. Strawberry benefits the spleen and pancreas, improves digestion and addresses sore throat and lung/bronchial issues. Strawberries are supportive to the urinary system and will assist in conditions associated with inflammation and the inability to urinate. Strawberries are rich in silicon and vitamin C, two nutrients essential for healing connective tissue and beautifying to the skin, hair and nails. Strawberries are a natural cleansing food as they promote elimination, build the blood and balance blood pressure. Strawberries contain vitamins A, C, B1, B2, B3 and the minerals calcium, phosphorus, magnesium, iron, sodium and potassium. Serving Size: 1 cup, Calories: 43, Protein: 1g, Carbs: 10g, Fat: 0g, Fiber: 3g

Tangerines are a rich source of vitamin C, foliate and beta-carotene. They also contain potassium, magnesium and vitamins B1, B2 & B3. Citrus fruits protect against infection and cancer. Serving Size: 1 large, Calories: 43g, Protein: 1g, Carbs 2g, Fat: 0g, Fiber: 2g

Made in the USA
Charleston, SC
14 July 2010